Dreamcatching

By Alan Siegel

Dreams That Can Change Your Life:
Navigating Life's Passages Through Turning-Point Dreams

By Kelly Bulkeley

An Introduction to the Psychology of Dreaming

Among All These Dreamers:
Essays on Dreaming and Modern Society

Spiritual Dreaming: A Cross-cultural and Historical Journey

The Wilderness of Dreams:
Exploring the Religious Meanings of Dreams in Modern Culture

Dreamcatching

EVERY PARENT'S GUIDE TO
EXPLORING AND UNDERSTANDING
CHILDREN'S DREAMS
AND NIGHTMARES

Alan Siegel, Ph.D.,

and Kelly Bulkeley, Ph.D.

THREE RIVERS PRESS/NEW YORK

ALAN SIEGEL
To Zoe and Sophia

KELLY BULKELEY
To Emilia "Tia" Zak

Published by Three Rivers Press, a division of Crown Publishers, Inc., 201 East 50th Street, New York, NY 10022. Member of the Crown Publishing Group.

Random House, Inc. New York, Toronto, London, Sydney, Auckland. http://www.randomhouse.com/

THREE RIVERS PRESS and colophon are trademarks of Crown Publishers, Inc.

Printed in the United States of America

Design by Lenny Henderson

Library of Congress Cataloging-in-Publication Data
Siegel, Alan B.
     Dreamcatching : every parent's guide to children's dreams and
  nightmares / by Alan Siegel and Kelly Bulkeley.
        p. cm.
     Includes bibliographical references.
     1. Children's dreams. 2. Dream interpretations. 3. Nightmares.
  I. Bulkeley, Kelly, 1962— II. Title.
  BF1099.CC55S54   1998
  154.6'3'083—dc21   97-23650
                                            CIP

ISBN 0-517-88788-6 (paperback)

10 9 8 7 6 5 4 3 2 1

First Edition

CONTENTS

ACKNOWLEDGMENTS

WE GRATEFULLY THANK THE CHILDREN AND PARENTS WHO contributed their dreams and nightmares, their life stories, and their time to our research.

Our agents, Ed Vesneske and Ling Lucas of Nine Muses and Apollo, shared a synchronistic inspiration about the need for this book and were instrumental in helping us refine our ideas in the early stages. Laura Wood and Leslie Meredith at Harmony shared our vision and provided crucial suggestions during the final stages. Thanks also to Laura for "catching" our title for us.

We want to thank our colleagues and friends at the Association for the Study of Dreams, who have been consistently generous with their personal and professional encouragement of our ideas and creativity. We also thank Shai Yerlick, whose Kensington Deli provided a nourishing environment for brainstorming sessions in the early stages of incubating this book.

ALAN SIEGEL'S ACKNOWLEDGMENTS

For incisive comments and consultation on the manuscript, I am grateful to my friends and colleagues, Saul Rosenberg, John Marron, Joanne Rochon, Deirdre Barrett, Ed Hoffman, Gary Stolzoff, Patrick Gannon, and my brother Bob Siegel. For additional support I also thank Joan Shimmamura, Bob Hoss, Rita Dwyer, and Clare McGorry.

I want to thank my family for their support and encouragement. My parents, Perle and Jerry Siegel, were not only vocal supporters but provided editorial help at every stage. My daughters, Zoe and Sophia, provided their dreams and their sense of wonder and creativity. Most of all, I thank my wife, Tracy, for generous emotional support and for reading and editing multiple versions of this tome.

KELLY BULKELEY'S ACKNOWLEDGMENTS

The teachers, students, and parents at the Association of Child Services in Oakland, California, the Kensington Nursery School in Kensington, California, and the Laboratory School in Chicago, Illinois, all have my deep gratitude for being so generous in sharing their dream lives with me. Educational consultant Lenore Thompson gave me valuable advice and encouragement at crucial stages of this project. Zosia Topolnicki and Elizabeth Bone of Apple Tree Childcare Center in El Cerrito, California, were a constant and friendly source of parenting wisdom, and I owe them thanks both for helping with the book and for caring so well for my daughter, Maya.

I thank my parents, Ned and Tish, my siblings, Michelle and Alex, my children, Dylan and Maya, and most of all my wife, Hilary, for the countless ways they supported me during the writing of the book. My deepest gratitude here goes to Emilia Zak. From her I learned the wonders, the mysteries, and the sheer hard work involved in nurturing the healthy growth of young children. More than anyone else, Tia Zak taught me the values that I've tried to express and honor in this work.

INTRODUCTION

WE ALL DREAM, EVERY NIGHT OF OUR LIVES. BEFORE YOUR children grow up and leave home, they will have had tens of thousands of dreams. And these dream images accurately reveal the essence of their fears, triumphs, and everyday concerns. If you encourage your children to remember and playfully explore their dreams, you will help them develop a lifelong access to heightened forms of creativity, intuition, insight, and emotional intelligence.

Dreamcatching provides a guided tour of the inner landscape of children's dreams and nightmares. Along the way, you will discover how to speak and understand the special language of dreaming, and how to connect each dream's story line to insights about how your children are coping with the events and challenges in their lives. We will demonstrate how the dreams of children mirror their worries about changes in the family brought on by the birth of a sibling, the move to a new home, the death of a grandparent, adoption, divorce, remarriage, and other life passages.[1]

You will learn to soothe and transform the pain of nightmares, to understand that disturbing dreams are a necessary part of regaining balance and smoothing out the emotional roller-coaster ride of change that occurs when illness, crisis, or trauma strike.

You will discover how children's dreams change and reflect the challenges of each stage of development—how monster and animal dreams highlight younger children's fears of the unknown, and how teenagers' dream characters reflect their need for acceptance and inclusion and their confusion about their developing identity.

Most important, you will learn simple techniques for encouraging your children to remember or "catch" their dreams, and family-friendly ways to talk to your children about their dreams without pressuring them. This unique form of sharing and exploration will increase your understanding of your children's deepest feelings and needs, and provide the opportunity for quality family communication.

Dreamcatching is built upon our experiences as parents, exploring dreams with our own children, and extensive work with the dreams of preschoolers, elementary-age children, and teens, as well as undergraduate and graduate students. Both Alan Siegel and Kelly Bulkeley began keeping dream journals as teenagers, and have used their own dreams for inner guidance for a combined total of forty-five years. In addition, Alan, a child psychologist, has more than twenty years of experience working with parents and children evaluating and resolving emotional difficulties and family transitions.

Not everyone in our society recognizes the value of children's dreaming and family dream-sharing. In fact, there are strong prejudices against talking with children about dreams. Even though psychologists have shown the many beneficial effects of dreaming on human development, even though cultures all around the world have made dream education a vital part of their children's upbringing, and even though many parents in our society have testified to the improvements they have experienced in family communication through dream-sharing, some of these prejudices remain. We hope this book reassures parents that making dreams a valued part of family conversations and activities is not only beneficial for children's emotional health, but it's also a vital way to help children trust and cultivate their intuition and open the powers of their imagination.

How to Use This Book

The dozens of dreams you'll read about are presented exactly as reported to us by children and parents. The names and some biographical details, however, have been changed to preserve the confidentiality of the dreamers and their families. The dreams were chosen from those reported by patients, workshop participants, research subjects, our own family members, and people we interviewed while collecting material for this book. Some of the dreams are drawn from other authors and researchers.

Please don't be concerned if the symbols and themes in your children's dreams don't match the examples we present, or if the dreams and explanations seem too clear-cut. We have tried to select dreams that are vivid, accessible to understanding, and broadly representative of different age groups and life situations. Although we have observed many universal themes in children's dreams, we strongly believe that the experiences and meanings of each individual's dreams are unique. Therefore, if your child's dreams don't fit the patterns we are describing, it may simply be a sign of his or her creativity and originality.

If you and your children are eager to get started remembering and exploring dreams, keeping a dream journal, creating art and writing projects based on your dreams, and learning to connect dream symbols to events in your child's life, turn to chapter eleven, "The Dream Catcher's Workbook." There you will find a Dream Catcher's Journal format designed especially for children. The chapter provides guidance on how to improve your ability to remember dreams, how to tell the story of your dreams, and how to listen and respond with empathy. In addition, you will find a cornucopia of dream-oriented techniques, exercises, and projects to help you unleash the creativity of your child's imagination.

For parents who have had anxiety dreams about their children or about the challenges of their role as a parent, chapter ten, "Your Dreams About Parenting," provides guidance and reassurance for handling different stages of the parenting cycle.

For preschool to high school teachers, counselors, youth and camp leaders, and learning specialists, there is a special appendix: "Every Teacher's Guide to Creative Dream Work for the Classroom." This highly practical supplement to "The Dream Catcher's Workbook" in chapter eleven provides additional creative exercises for exploring dreams in the classroom, in after-school and extracurricular activities, and at home.

A century ago, Belgian chemist Friedrich Kekulé von Stradonitz made the revolutionary discovery that the benzene molecule is structured in a ring, not a chain, after dreaming of a serpent biting his tail. In a speech to colleagues describing his discovery, he concluded: "Let us learn to dream, gentlemen, and then we may find the truth."[2] Inspired by Kekulé, we propose an anthem for the new millennium: "Let us teach our children to dream well!" Nascent in the imagination and dreams of our children are the creative breakthroughs of the future of humanity and the emotional resilience to navigate social pressures and renew our society.

1

THE FAMILY THAT
DREAMS TOGETHER

A S PARENTS LIVING IN A PRESSURED SOCIETY, WE ARE constantly searching for quality time with our children. Weary from busy careers, frightened by the violence and temptations that may derail our children from healthy development, many of us are eager to improve our ability to communicate with our sons and daughters. We want to guide them through the labyrinth of society's pressures, to help them assert their emotional needs and achieve their full creative, social, academic, and spiritual potential.

Dream-sharing offers a unique vehicle for making emotional and creative contact with our children. By sharing and exploring the images and the stories of dreams, children (and grown-ups) are expressing what is most vital in their minds and hearts.

Throughout the book, we will be recounting the stories of parents and children who have learned how to weave dream-sharing into their lives with wonderfully positive results. These stories demonstrate that there is nothing weird or mysterious about family members discussing and exploring dreams.

Ariel's Dream

On the second day of kindergarten, Ariel had a dream about a menacing unicorn that chased her on the way to school. By running through meadows and fields, she barely escaped and woke up frightened and anxious about getting ready for her new academic adventure. The dream was a surprise to Ariel's parents, as all summer she had been looking forward to "growing up" and entering kindergarten.

Being chased by an animal, monster, or imaginary creature is probably the most common type of dream remembered by young children. Yet for Ariel, a unicorn was not just any monster. It happened to be the name of her preschool, where, for three years, she had thrived socially and academically and felt emotionally safe. Despite her conscious excitement about starting kindergarten, unconsciously, Ariel was unsettled about the thought of a new school with unknown teachers, classrooms, and kids. The image of a unicorn, which had represented safety and creativity during preschool, could no longer be trusted. Its horn and its magical power to fly had become an incarnation of her fears of the unknown.

Understanding the meaning of the unicorn image was reassuring and orienting to Ariel's parents. Without further explanation from Ariel, and without any expert interpretation, the telling of the dream revealed that her excitement was tempered with normal fears, which she was trying to suppress. Once her fears were more visible to her parents, they could offer more guidance about how to fend off dream unicorns and how to make friends and get adjusted to kindergarten.

Welcoming the Dream

"Welcoming the dream" is an attitude of accepting any dream no matter how brief, confusing, or frightening it may be. Every dream, even those that seem utterly bizarre, can be a stimulus for creative exploration. By inviting children to share their dreams and validating the unique products of their imaginations, you can build your children's self-esteem.

So fluff up your child's pillow and roll out the imaginary red carpet. With parental encouragement, curiosity, and a welcoming attitude, children will begin to feel comfortable and their dreams will flow—with stories emerging like newborns from the womb of their imagination. Like a midwife attending a birth, you can catch these dreams, embrace them in an emotional security blanket, and nurture your child's tender, creative images and narratives with your excitement and encouragement.

When grown-ups treat dreams as important and worthy of discussion, children begin to pay attention to their dreams and remember them more often. Simple encouragement is often all it takes. However, if dream recall is blocked, there are some tried-and-true remedies for both kids and adults.

First and foremost, try to refrain from pressuring children—too much pressure can sour them on dream-sharing. You don't want to turn dreaming into a competition, or show disappointment if your child is not a good dream recaller. For kids who tend to have performance anxieties, indirect approaches may work better than direct encouragement. Quality over quantity should be a prevailing principle.

When dreams become a part of everyday conversations and kids hear their parents or older siblings discussing dreams, even if only occasionally, they become curious and will want to join in and emulate the older family members. When Alan's two-and-a-half-year-old daughter Sophia heard her older sister telling a scary dream about a fire, and saw her mom and dad listening intently, she did not want to be left out. She began to declare that she "had a dream, too!" when she would wake from a nap or in the morning. Her eagerness to be like her sister resulted in her parents hearing many fascinating dreams, and some waking fantasies as well.

Sharing Dreams Is Sharing Feelings

Dreams frequently express feelings that are too over-whelming for children to put into words. Relating a dream, therefore, opens a crucial channel of communication between parents and their children. Describing the characters and activities of a dream allows a child to express worries and even joys in a safer format than through direct verbal expression. For example, most children of divorce regularly fantasize and dream that their parents are reunited. These dreams may arise when events in waking life remind them of some painful aspects of the divorce. For parents who had hoped these poignant wishes would fade with time, it may be demoralizing to hear these dreams. However, the dreams and fantasies provide parents with an important alert that issues are surfacing that need to be addressed with gentle inquiry and reassurance.

When eight-year-old Danielle's grandmother made fun

of her speech impediment, she awoke in the middle of the night with a terrifying dream.

ANGRY FIRE DARTS

A person from a cartoon show was getting yelled at for doing lots of things the wrong way. She became angry and starting throwing lots of darts with fire on them. They landed on the ground and people were crying and afraid they would get burned. There was a doctor there who said maybe he could help me put out all the fires from the darts.

As Danielle's mother, Julie, reflected on her daughter's frightening dream, she realized how vulnerable Danielle was to her grandmother's ridicule. For Julie, the fire darts highlighted Danielle's angry frustration at her own inadequacies, and her speech problem made it seem to Danielle that something was wrong with her in the eyes of others. Although Julie did not interpret or explain the dream to Danielle, this dream was a turning point for Julie. The Fire Dart dream increased her awareness of her daughter's sensitivity to criticism and motivated her to talk with her mother, urging her to be more gentle and reassuring toward her granddaughter. For Julie, it also reawakened childhood memories of how her mother had been harsh with her and how painful that had been.

Although Julie and her husband had provided Danielle with excellent speech therapy that had been quite helpful, the dream made Julie more aware of the emotional side effects of having a disability. She resolved to focus on building Danielle's self-esteem and shielding her from unnecessary criticism.

Dream Sharing Is a Two-Way Street

Parents may be surprised to find that when they share their own dreams with their children, they receive remarkable and insightful responses. Kelly mentioned a dream he'd had to his five-year-old son, Dylan, and he got an unexpected response.

DISCOVERY ON JUPITER

I'm going with a group of scientists to one of Jupiter's moons, where a skull from an alien species had been found. I'm very excited at the chance to join such a history-making exploration.

Kelly shared the dream with Dylan while they were reading a book on space exploration. Dylan was fascinated by the dream and began asking a series of questions. "Were there any more people alive on the moon?" "Were you scared, Dad?" "Would the other people on the moon get mad that you and the scientists were taking the skull, and the moon people might still want to remember the dead person and keep the skull?"

By sharing his own curiosity and emotional experience of the dream, Dylan stimulated valuable insights for his father. Kelly became more aware of his own fears in the dream and began thinking about the symbolic image of grave-robbing. Dylan felt proud that he had helped his dad figure out some things about the dream. The exchange made Dylan feel more comfortable about telling his parents more about his own scary dreams.

Through the parent-child communication that occurs in family dream-sharing, children feel understood and reassured when they are challenged by new feelings, events, and relationships. Children also feel appreciated for their creativity and uniqueness. And parents attain greater awareness and understanding of important feelings that their child may not be able to express verbally. They may even get advance warning about issues that are troubling their child, such as frustration with schoolwork, the impact of a bully at school, or psychological residue from a divorce.

Through dream exploration, parents increasingly reflect upon their effectiveness in parenting and can make needed changes. They also gain understanding of their child's newly developing capacities, and they may even gain insights into their own childhood or current life.

How Your Own Dreams Can Enhance Your Parenting Skills

When Michael was eight, he had a recurring nightmare of being bounced around like a kernel of popcorn trapped in an electric popper. At the time, he sought comfort in his parents' bed, but they seemed preoccupied and grumpy and told him "don't worry, it's just a dream." Thirty years later, he was still puzzled about his dream and occasionally had nightmares with a similar feeling of tumbling, falling, and losing control.

During a children's dream workshop, the children were encouraged to draw pictures of their dreams, and Michael and the other parents were encouraged to draw their own earliest remembered dream. Some parents grumbled about this request, but Michael was intrigued with the idea. He grabbed the colored markers and made a series of quick sketches of the popcorn kernels whirling, like frenetic dancers caught in a tornado.

Childhood dreams are pregnant with psychological and artistic possibilities. As Michael sketched the dream, he was surprised at how he was instantaneously transported back in time. He had not thought about that difficult period in his life for many years. Or perhaps, he had tried to forget the fact that he attended eight different schools before graduating from high school.

Growing up, Michael had plenty of comforts and was never abused or mistreated, but he often felt lonely, with no one to turn to. His father, a U.S. Foreign Service officer who was frequently transferred, seemed irritable all the time, and his mother seemed always to be paying attention to his baby sister.

In the days after the workshop, Michael had more flash-backs, and he began to see how well the dream's metaphor expressed the insecurity of his childhood. During those years, he had literally and emotionally been bounced around like a popcorn kernel—moving, losing friends; changing schools, countries, and even languages with little preparation. It's not that his parents were unsympathetic, but they were often overwhelmed themselves and couldn't provide reassurance when Michael felt abandoned and withdrew.

Not long after the dream workshop, Michael was offered a job promotion that involved extensive travel and more frequent relocation. He was tempted by the money and benefits of the new position, but found himself having a recurring dream about riding recklessly in a late 1960s Chevy Impala, like the one his dad used to own. The anxious feeling he had upon waking reminded him of his drawings of the furiously spinning popcorn kernels. After the third night of having this dream, Michael decided not to accept the new job. He was determined not to subject his own son, Aaron, to the emotional tumult of relocating that had troubled Michael as a child.

Inspired by how drawing his dream had helped him to understand key events in his childhood, Michael began to keep a Dream Catcher's Journal and even started one for Aaron, so his son would have a record of his own childhood dreams along with his photo albums and other precious mementos.

Childhood dreams, preserved like amber in our psyche, are jewels waiting to be discovered. Each time we review and explore our childhood dreams we find something new —the exhilaration of flying to avoid being captured by pirates, or the dread of quaking in fear of the fierce monsters and snakes who used to live under your bed. Often the symbols in childhood dreams are repeated and continue to have relevance later in life.

The two best ways to help guide your children with their dreams are to invite them to talk about their dreams and to remember and explore your own. The optimal starting point is to try to remember any dreams or nightmares you may have had as a child.

What can we learn from our own childhood dreams? As parents, exploring early dreams opens up new insights as to the challenges we faced in childhood. Reflecting on early dreams can illuminate how we attempted to cope with life-changing events such as moving, the birth of a sibling, illness in the family, or the first day of school.

Most psychotherapies underscore the value of exploring childhood events and relationships as a vital source of insight into present behaviors. Areas where we were emotionally wounded as children tend to persist into adulthood, and have a tremendous influence (sometimes unconsciously) on the way we parent.

Pondering your own childhood dreams and experiences can help you understand the emotional climate of your family of origin. The insights you gain allow you to respect and nourish the uniqueness of your children and differentiate their experiences from your own. Being clear on where your feelings end and your child's feelings begin is a crucial skill of parenting.

Why do we forget most dreams but remember a few for a lifetime? Long-remembered dreams from childhood usually date back to watershed events and key periods of development. At workshops, when parents are invited to share their early dreams, many date back to ages four through seven, the time when children face the developmental challenges of entering preschool, kindergarten, or grade school. This stage of development is both exciting and stressful and involves separating more from parents and learning new social and academic skills. Vivid dreams and nightmares are a vital part of coping with these new experiences.

It is not unusual for a childhood dream symbol to continue intermittently for years or even decades and to take on a wide range of story lines often united by a common emotion such as threat or abandonment. Alan's daughter Zoe was two when the Oakland/Berkeley firestorm burned three thousand houses within a couple of miles of her home. Despite attempts to shield her viewing habits, she ended up seeing the frightening flames and destruction on television, and friends who were threatened by the fire stayed at her house until all the flames were put out.

Variations on Zoe's fire dreams have recurred intermittently during times of major and minor stress and tend to symbolize various kinds of worries that may or may not be directly related to actual fire danger. When she was almost eight years old, a family discussion of home safety procedures in case of fire provoked another terrifying fire dream, one that involved desperately attempting to rescue her little sister from a raging house fire. Talking about her nightmare helped calm her anxieties and led to further fruitful discussions about fire safety and how to deal with worries in general.

Although the vulnerabilities in children's dreams may be more acute and the symbolism more transparent when compared with the dreams of adults, the underlying themes are similar. In fact, it is not unusual for children and adults to share certain dream and nightmare symbols across generations. In one family, both the father and the son suffered from the nightmare of being attacked by wolves, and the father had never discussed this dream with his son.

Sharing your childhood dreams and nightmares with your children will pique their interest and normalize the experience of dreaming, so they will be more enthusiastic and want to emulate your ability to recall dreams. When they hear that you, too, had monster nightmares and had to cower in your mother's arms for protection, they will feel less isolated and intimidated by their own nightmares. Exploring your early dreams increases your awareness and understanding of your children's dream experiences. You may even want to keep your own dream journal or join your child in the activities described. It's not only informative but great family fun.

Guidelines for Family Dream-Sharing

Our work draws on contemporary theories of child development and years of practical experience guiding children
and parents in their exploration of dreams and nightmares.
We have harvested insights from psychological and anthro-
pological research on dreams, psychotherapy with children,
and expressive arts therapies in synthesizing our family-
oriented approach to dream exploration. Based on those
sources, we offer the following family dream-sharing
guidelines.

- Welcome the sharing of dreams. Take the time to listen
  carefully and sympathetically to each other's dreams,
  feelings, and reactions.
- Offer words of reassurance and a soothing emotional
  presence to vulnerable children suffering nightmares.
- Nourish the creative spark in each family member's
  dreams, encourage everyone to take the images and
  stories seriously and express them through writing,
  drama, and other art forms.
- Help each child imagine solutions for the worries and
  challenges that emerge as a focus in dreams.

Six-year-old Zack had a terrifying dream of two monsters fighting and biting each other. He had completed one
week of the Dream Catcher's Journal (see chapter eleven
for details), writing down, with the help of his parents, as
many dreams as he could remember. When he awoke in
tears and told his parents the nightmare, his father, Lenny,
realized that Zack's dream was probably related to the
argument about family finances that he and his wife had

had the previous evening. Lenny quickly offered this explanation to Zack, saying, "those monsters are probably symbols of me and Mommy fighting last night." While Lenny's explanation is probably accurate, Zack was not comforted. He said, "No, Daddy! Those monsters were not you and Mommy. They were scary and they acted like they might kill me, too." When Lenny repeated another variation of his interpretation, Zack just continued to cry and refused to discuss any other dreams for weeks afterward.

Both children and adults are sensitive to having their dreams prematurely explained. Many children will even stop remembering or reporting dreams, as Zack did, if they feel their dreams are being overanalyzed or dissected. Zack probably would have benefited more from emotional and physical comforting at the time of the dream than he did from his father's explanation.

It can be liberating for parents to learn they don't have to analyze or classify their children's dreams. It is also empowering when parents realize that their own intuition, imagination, and knowledge of their child is just as crucial as how many books they have read on dream analysis.

Especially for younger children, premature verbal interpretation may be inhibiting, and may lead them to become more protective and secretive about their dreams. So use your intuition and insights into dreams to sense areas where your child may be stressed by events or relationships. However, don't get too carried away with formal explanations and interpretations of dream symbols.

In contrast to interpretation techniques, the approach of "dreaming the dream onward" emphasizes reexperiencing parts of the dream using fantasy and creative expression. Often the simplest techniques can be the most rewarding.

This could include allowing a dream character to speak using puppets or action figures, playacting a new and more resolved ending for a dream, sketching or painting a dream image, or using the appearance of a dream adversary to talk about how to defend oneself in an emergency situation.

At the heart of dreaming the dream onward is play— freewheeling, mischievous, frolicking, poetic play. So when your child tells you a dream about flying, the theme of the dream may relate to a sense of exhilaration, freedom, feeling above it all or even flying too high. We recommend deferring these possible explanations and, instead, helping children concentrate on the *experience* of flying in its many forms. Younger children may want to mimic the sounds and motions of the plane as they fly around the room. Older children may sketch the plane, photograph an air show, imagine they are astronauts, or remember times they have flown to visit their grandparents or met people at the airport. Every memory, idea, or association to the metaphor of flying will illuminate the dream and expand its range of meanings.

We like the aesthetic of pioneer dream researcher Montague Ullman, who coined the term *dream appreciation*[1] to suggest that the most fertile freeways for dream exploration are those that feature creative expression, curious exploration, and a savoring of the ever-changing vistas of the imagination.

2

THE PLAYFUL CREATIVITY
OF CHILDREN'S DREAMS

I F THERE IS ONE SINGLE GOAL THAT MOST PARENTS have for raising their children, it is to nurture a rich capacity for creativity. No matter what our children grow up to be—doctors or teachers, gardeners or cooks, astronauts or architects—their lives will be enhanced by a strong, well-developed ability to be creative: to imagine new potentials and possibilities; to envision alternative solutions to difficult problems; and to joyfully express their own unique hopes and desires for the world.

This passionate desire to do all they can to stimulate the growth of their children's creativity leads parents to push their children into a variety of elaborate, and often very expensive, activities. Some parents buy their children an art studio's worth of paints, drawing materials, and craft supplies. Other parents enroll their children in special classes at museums and science centers, where experts can give the children personal instruction. And still other parents send their children to private camps for even more specialized instruction in music, dance, computers, sports, and dozens of other activities.

Although all of these efforts are well intentioned, they

may have the unintended side effect of making children feel so pressured by parental expectations that they can't have any real fun with the activities. Ironically, the very attempt to stimulate their children can end up robbing them of the ability to freely and spontaneously explore their inclinations.

We have a suggestion for parents who want to provide the best possible support for their children's budding creative spirits: look to their dreams. Dreams don't cost any money, you don't have to drive anywhere to find them, you don't have to fit them into your calendar, and you don't have to assemble them or install any batteries. The creative energies of children's dreams flow naturally and freely every night; all you need is a bit of patience and a sense of adventure to help your children learn how to draw upon this truly infinite fountain of spontaneous expression.

Dreams and Creative Inspiration in History

Throughout history, dreams have been recognized as a vital source of inspiration. In religion, science, and the arts, dreams have provided people with valuable sparks of insight that have led to the creation of new paintings, inventions, religious rituals, and works of music. History contains abundant evidence that dreaming is, in a very literal sense, the essence of human creativity.

Writer Robert Louis Stevenson said he first came up with the plot of his story *Dr. Jekyll and Mr. Hyde* in a dream. Artist and poet William Blake regularly drew on his dreams for creative energy, and titled one of his portraits "The Man Who Taught Blake Painting in His Dreams." Inventor Elias Howe came up with his novel sewing machine design—

running the thread through a hole at the tip of the needle—after having a nightmare in which he was a prisoner of cannibals who happened to be holding spears with holes at their pointy tips. Philosopher René Descartes had a series of life-changing dreams in his early twenties that inspired him to write his revolutionary philosophical theories. Filmmakers like Akira Kurosawa, Francis Ford Coppola, Ingmar Bergman, Robert Altman, and John Sayles have all put images and themes from their dreams into their movies.[1]

Naomi Epel's book *Writers Dreaming* offers some particularly striking examples of dream-inspired creativity in the works of some of today's most important writers.[2] Here is Isabelle Allende's account of how dreams have influenced her novels:

> I write in a very organic way. Books don't happen in my mind, they happen somewhere in my belly. It's like a long elephant pregnancy that can last two years. . . . With *House of the Spirits*, my first novel, I knew how the book would end, I knew what I wanted to say and I knew why I had written it. Still, I had written the last fifteen pages more than ten times and I could never get it right. It was solemn, preachy—too political, melodramatic. I couldn't get the tone. One night, at three o'clock in the morning, I woke up with a dream. In the dream my grandfather was lying on his bed . . . , dressed in black on his black bed. Everything was black in the room except the white sheets. I was sitting on a black chair, dressed in black, and I was telling him that I had written this book and what the book was about. So, when I woke up from the dream, I realized that I had been telling this story to

my grandfather all the time. The tone of the whole book was his voice and my voice talking. And I realized then that the end of the book, naturally, would be that the grandfather has died and the granddaughter is waiting for dawn to bury him. So the epilogue has the tone of a person sitting beside her grandfather, who is dead, sitting by his bed, telling the story very simply. The dream gave me that.[3]

Whether or not your children become world-famous writers, artists, philosophers, and inventors, their powers of imagination can be greatly enhanced and stimulated by learning how to pay attention to their dreams. When we dream, our mind relaxes. The control of our conscious ego disappears, and a different way of thinking takes over, what psychologists call "primary process thinking." This nonrational way of thinking allows for the free exploration of possibilities and the spontaneous emergence of original ideas. Particularly when we are facing a difficult problem in waking life, our dreaming mind literally plays with the problem, turning it over and over again, looking at it from different perspectives, trying out different solutions.

Most dreams that children remember are nightmares, because those are the dreams that awaken them most suddenly and dramatically. However, the sleep laboratory research of psychologist David Foulkes and others indicates that, in fact, the majority of children's dreams are pleasant, with themes of being adventurous, powerful, playful, and affectionate.[4] Because of our culture's taboo on taking dreams seriously ("Oh, it's just a dream"), children tend to remember only their scary dreams. Yet when all their dreams are treated as special and recall is welcomed, children begin remembering their positive dreams and develop a deeper appreciation for the creative powers inherent within all their dreaming experiences.

Every dream, no matter how foolish or trivial it may appear, is a product of the child's emerging capacity to create, to imagine, to make sense of the world and his or her place within it. Even very frightening dreams and nightmares usually turn out to be, on closer inspection, expressions of tremendous creativity.

First Dreams and Career Visions

One of the most remarkable stories we have encountered in our research on children's dreams is that of a boy named Ben. The youngest child in his family, Ben grew up watching his two older brothers race up and down the driveway on their bicycles. Ben eagerly awaited the day when he would be big enough to have his own bike and be allowed to ride around by himself. Finally, for his fifth birthday, Ben got a bike and started learning how to ride it—very slowly and carefully at first, but soon with increasing skill and independence. During this exciting time Ben had two dreams:

THE GOLDEN BICYCLE
I see a golden bicycle, with glowing golden light from behind. It's a ten-speed road bike, and it glows.

RIDING ON A SEA OF CATS
I'm riding a bike, and the ground is covered with cats; it's like a sea of cats, cats as far as I can see; there are so many of them I can't see the ground

beneath them. I'm worried about riding my bike on top of them, because they might get angry at me and attack me; and there are so many of them that if they did I'd be in real trouble. But then I notice that my bike's tires are made of soft, padded cotton gloves, like a ring of hands with the palms facing outwards; so when I ride over the cats they are patted and stroked by the gloves.

As Ben got older, his fascination with bicycles grew ever deeper. Beginning at age seven he became a bike racer, competing in dirt-bike races. Before starting college he took some time off and created a small company that manufactured specially designed bicycle brakes. After he graduated from college, Ben went to work for a major bicycle manufacturer, doing research and development on the company's newest lines of bikes. Today he is still at that company, helping to design some of the most sophisticated, high-tech bicycles available on the market.

Ben says his two bicycle dreams became a powerful source of inspiration throughout his childhood and young adulthood, motivating him to carefully nurture what was to him the spiritual meaning of bicycles. The golden light radiating from the bike in the first dream reminded him of religious portraits he had seen in church, with the haloes of light surrounding the head of Jesus; this, for Ben, emphasized the liberating power of bikes in his life. The "sea of cats" in the second dream brought to mind the family cat, who had just had a litter of kittens around the time of the two dreams. This second dream reinforced the message that young Ben's parents had been trying to get across to him, that he had to be very careful not to accidentally harm the kittens as he excitedly zoomed around on his bike.

These two dreams foreshadowed, in remarkably accurate terms, what would be the greatest passion and most creative pursuit of Ben's life. From those early days when he enviously watched his older brothers in the driveway, bikes represented freedom and independence to Ben. As he got older he found that the powerful rhythm of pedaling, the balance he learned to maintain over bumps and through turns, the focused concentration on the road ahead, the deep, lung-filling breathing, and the total control he had over his speed and destination all combined to make bicycle riding the most passionate activity in his life. Ben's two childhood dreams provided him with a profoundly inspiring vision of what bicycles would always mean to him.

Of course, not all childhood dreams offer such striking anticipations of a child's future life vocation. But the creative power of dreaming is such that some childhood dream experiences do indeed provide visions of future directions in life—pointing toward future potentials and horizons.

When he was four years old, Paul dreamed repeatedly that two giant monsters were chasing him with a vacuum cleaner. Paul was sucked into the vacuum cleaner and suddenly felt as if he was in outer space, where all sense of proportion and direction was gone. Paul went on to become a brilliant astrophysicist, developing theoretical models of complex spatial relationships. As an adult, Paul realized with wonder that all of his academic research was essentially aimed at solving the conceptual problems that were first raised in his childhood dreams of floating freely in the vastness of outer space. Paul, who had always suffered from periodic bouts of paralyzing anxiety, came to see that the two giant monsters in his dreams represented his parents: Their frequent yelling and arguing during his early childhood had frightened him terribly, making him feel lonely, abandoned, "lost in space." As he grew up, Paul studied spatial characteristics in math, science, and finally astrophysics. Just as he struggled to respond to the fearful emotions of his childhood dreams, he devoted his life work to exploring and mastering the nature of space in the universe.

Bob was five years old when his father was forced to leave home for military service. Although his mother always remained nurturing and dependable, Bob was acutely aware of how much stress she was under, having to take care of the children, the house, the finances, and everything else. Soon after his father's departure, Bob started kindergarten, and it was a disaster: he had no friends, he hated his teacher, and he got in several fistfights that led to reprimands from the school's principal. Finally, his mother moved him to another school. During this terribly unsettled time in his young life, Bob started having dreams of tornadoes:

THE TORNADO IS COMING

The dreams always start out with me in the front yard of my house and playing with a group of other kids. Then we look up and see a big, black storm coming in the sky. All the other kids run inside their houses, but I can't run; my legs won't work and the storm is filling the sky—and I wake up in terror.

As Bob shared his tornado dreams with his mother, she realized that they were expressing Bob's feelings about their family's "stormy" situation, and his fear that he can't "get inside the house" and find the same protection and comfort that other children receive from their families during times of stress and trouble. As they talked, Bob's fears subsided, and he became increasingly curious about the powerful forces of nature that his tornado dreams were revealing to him. The next time the dream came, something new happened:

THE COLORFUL STORM

I'm out in the yard, playing with the other kids like in the other dreams. But this time, when the storm comes, and all the kids start running away, I remember that I'm in a dream, and I stop running. I turn around, and look up in the sky, and suddenly I see the storm turn into all these beautiful colors and patterns: spirals, squares, and circles, like dazzling little rainbows. I'm still afraid, but I'm also amazed by the colors filling the sky.

Bob became increasingly interested in dreams, and in colors. He began conducting his own personal experiments, pressing the sides of his eyes and observing the colorful geometric patterns that would result. Things began to go better for Bob at his new school, and although he still missed his father and worried about his mother, he felt a new sense of emotional strength that could help him "weather the storms." He had one more tornado dream:

THE LAST TORNADO DREAM

I'm in the same dream, and this time when I see the storm approaching I actually want it to come. It's so beautiful and the colors and patterns are so interesting that I don't want to wake up.

We will talk more about Bob's other interesting childhood dreams in other chapters. For now, we simply want to mention that later in his life, after a successful business career involving light and laser technology, Bob devoted himself to a careful and systematic study of the nature of color. Prompted in large part by the "tornado dreams" of his early childhood, he sustained a strong interest in dreams and began teaching people about the symbolism of color in dreams. In these ways Bob found a creative outlet by which he could share with other people the incredible feelings of awe and mystery he felt in those childhood dreams.

We believe that examples like these should inspire parents to pay especially close attention to the very first dreams their children remember. In tribal cultures all over the world, a child's first dreams are greeted by the elders as revelations of the child's future destiny—as a great hunter, perhaps, or a wise prophet, or a powerful healer. Whatever the particular message of the dream, the elders always encourage the child to remember the dream and keep it close to his or her heart, as a special sign of the unique talents and abilities that will unfold as the child grows older.

Our goal is to encourage parents in today's society to pay this kind of careful attention to their children's dreams, helping them learn how to recognize, appreciate, and express the wonderful creative energies that emerge through their dreaming experiences.

Dreams and Creative Breakthroughs

Fourteen-year-old Brady had recently formed a band with some of his friends. Despite some parental resistance, Brady and his friends were passionately committed to their band, and they practiced long hours together in the garage at one of the boys' homes. When the band had finally gotten good enough to play in public, they arranged to perform at a school dance. As the date of the dance approached, and as the pressure of schoolmates looking forward to hearing the band increased, Brady tried to perfect his playing of a certain guitar section in one of the band's best songs. But no matter how many hours he worked at it, he just couldn't figure out how to improve his playing of that one frustrating section. Then one night, after he had spent all evening trying, and failing, to get the song right, Brady went to sleep and had a dream.

> PLAYING THE SONG PERFECTLY
> *I have my guitar, and I'm playing the song perfectly—*
> *I can see, with total clarity, my fingers moving up*
> *and down the fret board, using a technique I've never*
> *tried in my waking practice. I'm so amazed I've*
> *finally gotten the song right!*

When he woke up the next morning Brady immediately grabbed his guitar, tried out the technique he had used in his dream, and got it right the very first time. The night of the big dance finally arrived, and the band's debut performance went pretty well. Although Brady did mess up during a couple of songs, he played that one song from his dream perfectly.

Children usually have less trouble than adults do in tapping into that free-flowing, "primary process" mode of thinking found in dreaming. What parents should focus on is helping their children not forget their innate capacity for spontaneous creative thought and imagination. Growing up in a society that so heavily emphasizes logic and rationality, today's children often assume that becoming an adult means abandoning their love of playing, imagining, and dreaming. We believe, however, that the goal of any child's development should be to integrate logical thought with dreaming imagination. Brady's story illustrates just such an integration. He never would have kept playing guitar (over his parents' objections) if it weren't for the "non-rational" passion and enjoyment he got from it. And he never would have gotten very good at playing if he hadn't practiced for long hours, working very hard to learn musical theory. And then, he never would have taken the next step to a new level of skill and enjoyment if his dreams hadn't given him a timely dose of creative inspiration and technical advice.

Are They Just Making It Up?

THE SHARK AT THE BEACH

I was at a beach, and all my friends were there, and we were playing with a ball. . . . Then suddenly, a shark came out of the water, and tried to bite the ball. . . . And then, Wonder Woman came, and she chased the shark away. . . . And Wonder Woman was our friend, and gave us all gold medals. . . . Then we all got on top of a whale and rode around the ocean, and had some ice cream, and went to Disneyland.

If a child wakes up in the morning and says this is what she just dreamed, how is a parent to know if it's really a dream, or if the child is just making some (or all) of it up? Many parents have asked us if it's ever possible to be sure that what their children report as a dream isn't in fact just a fantasy, a pretend story, or a retelling of a plot from a book or video.

Our view is that fantasies, dreams, and even stories shared by children are important and should be taken seriously. We recommend that parents not worry about how to define the experience, and focus instead on listening carefully to the emotions and feelings their children are expressing in what they themselves are calling a "dream." One important consequence of looking at children's dreams as a kind of play is that the emphasis shifts from rational explanation to imaginative expression. Instead of worrying about how to categorize their children's experiences, parents should ask non-goal-directed questions such as What was it like? How did it feel? and What happened next?

There are, of course, some pretty clear signs that usually indicate when children are embellishing their dream reports. A change in their voices, a different look on their faces, the appearance of obviously fanciful characters and events are indicators that children have stopped reporting the dream and have begun adding new elements. In "The Shark at the Beach," for example, a parent might suspect that the "real" dream goes as far as the shark biting the ball, and maybe includes the arrival of Wonder Woman, but after that, it sounds like pieces of waking fantasy are being woven into the narrative.

Even if parents think they can detect signs of embellishment in their children's dream reports, we still recommend that they keep this to themselves, and just focus on the children's emotions and feelings. Kelly learned this lesson the hard way when he was talking one day with a kindergarten class about their dreams. He was sitting with a five-year-old girl named Claire, and he asked her if she remembered any of her dreams. Claire answered yes, she very clearly remembered "a scary dream":

THE BABY GIRL PONY

There's a baby girl pony, with blue eyes and blond hair and pink and purple fur. A monster comes, with brown hair, and puts the pony in the trash. Then he wants to cut the baby pony with a saw. But then the monster and the pony become friends. They lived at the pony's house. The mommy pony says, "Who's that?" The monster scares the baby pony again by growling, but then they're friends again. Then the monster carries the baby pony away, and touches her hair. The mommy pony says, "Don't poke my baby pony." Then the monster didn't live with her. There was a dragon living next door, a baby monster and a baby dragon. The monster takes its costume off, and says, "I'm your father, and I'm going to be your friend!" Then the father wasn't my friend anymore, and the animals grew up. Then, one day, . . .

For the next fifteen minutes or so Claire continued to relate in elaborate, increasingly complex detail the thrilling adventures of the baby girl pony. When she finally finished Kelly thanked her for sharing such a wonderful story with him. "It wasn't a story," Claire angrily replied. "It was a dream!" She turned away from Kelly and refused to talk to him for the rest of the afternoon.

So much for adult categories and analyses! The adventures of the baby girl pony clearly expressed Claire's emotional troubles with her father, who had recently divorced her mother and was now living in a different house. Kelly's comment, though well intentioned, inadvertently ignored the feelings that Claire was expressing through her narrative. She took the comment as an insult to her abilities to describe her own experiences. In talking with children about their dreams, this point can never be overemphasized: Always let the child's feelings be the guide.

Dream Games

There are many, many different ways to express the creative energies that emerge in our dreams. One way that is particularly enjoyable for children is to make a game out of dreaming—getting together with some friends to create a little space in waking life for the playfulness of dreams to be shared, explored, and celebrated.

Four boys run outside into their nursery school's backyard, climbing onto a play structure warmed by the morning sun. Aaron, the regular leader of this little gang, suddenly declares, "It's bedtime." The other boys immediately lie down on the play structure and pretend to go to sleep. But a few moments later, Bruce, who is "number two" in the gang and sometimes struggles with Aaron for control over their play, starts growling while he lies with his eyes closed. Aaron sits up and says, "No, don't do any growling," but Bruce says, "It's just a dream." "Yeah," Aaron quickly agrees, "this is a dream. Come on!" He leads the other boys off the structure, and they all start growling and stalking around the yard in exaggerated "dream" motions. The teachers in the yard observe this boisterous play with some skepticism, but they don't say anything. Then Bruce shouts, "There's fire in my dream," and he starts kicking out at it "like a karate guy." "There's fire in my dream, too," Aaron shouts, and starts doing his own karate kicks, as do the two other boys, Joe and Manuel. Again, the teachers are clearly disapproving, but because the boys are not threatening anyone in particular, they allow the "dream" to go on. After several minutes of vigorous dream-fighting, Aaron calls out, "Now, Bruce, we wake up!" "OK!" Bruce says, and they all hurry back up to the play structure. They lie down again for a few moments, then "wake up."

Although these boys are only four years old, they are exploring and clarifying the differences between dreaming and waking behaviors. By pretending to be in a "dream," they are able to play more freely and to express aggressive urges more vigorously than their teachers would ordinarily allow. The boys are, in effect, turning the common adult refrain "it's only a dream" back on the grown-ups, and using it as a kind of cover for their play. The game also gives Bruce a chance to express more openly his desires to be a leader in their group; and in this "dream" context, Aaron is more willing than usual to share his leadership with someone else, and to enjoy that experience.

Dream games may spontaneously emerge any time a group of children get together to play. Such games may also be more deliberately organized, with a more elaborate set of rules and parts for people to play.

A remarkable example of this is the Dream Guessing Game, which the Iroquois people of the Great Lakes have been performing for over three hundred years at their annual midwinter festival.[5] In this game, members of the tribe try to guess each other's dreams, which are presented in the form of riddles. For example, the dreamer might say to the others, "It whistled in the wind," to refer to a dream of a corn husk spirit, or "It has holes, yet it catches," about a dream of a lacrosse stick net. Everyone in the audience eagerly tries to figure out the meaning of these clever and often very humorous riddles. Whoever correctly guesses the riddle then promises to give the dreamer the dream item in question, and the dreamer in turn gives the guesser a small gift as thanks. The Dream Guessing Game continues for three nights until all the dream riddles have been successfully solved. Although there is a playful atmosphere of joy and celebration throughout the three nights, the Iroquois take very seriously the promise to give the dreamers whatever it is they have dreamed. An early Christian missionary who visited the Iroquois and watched them play this game filed an amazed report with his superiors in 1636:

> One man dreamed that he must have a canoe, eight beavers, two [sting]rays, six score gull's eggs, a turtle, and a man who would adopt him as his son; just think, what a fancy! . . . Indeed he had no sooner recited his dream than the old people of the village met to talk it over. They set about finding what he had asked with as much care and eagerness as if it had

been a question of preserving the whole Country; the Captain's father adopted him as his son, everything he had dreamed was given to him, the same day; as for the gull's eggs, they were changed into as many small loaves, which kept busy all the women of the village.

In today's society, the only "game" most adults play with their dreams is to make lighthearted fun of them at cocktail parties. "You wouldn't believe the strange dream I had last night!" someone might say, and then proceed to share the dream to polite smiles and laughter. There's nothing wrong with this, such conversations are often very entertaining. But as dream games go, it's pretty tame stuff. It's as if we grown-ups were given a deck of cards and were content to play Go Fish while our kids follow tribal cultures and use their decks to play hearts, bridge, and poker.

Dreaming Is Play

In the rest of this book we show parents various ways of understanding their children's dreams as profoundly meaningful expressions of feelings about family, friends, school experiences, and other aspects of their young lives. But as we do that, we want to make sure that parents never forget the simple playfulness of their children's dreams—and the fact that dreaming is a natural expression of a child's emerging capacities for imaginative play.

Actually, the connection between dreaming and play is surprisingly strong. Researchers who have studied play behaviors in humans and other animal species have found that play is autotelic—that is, it is carried out for its own sake, without being directed toward or motivated by any exterior goals. Play involves the creation of an "unreal" or "quasi-real" space, a special area clearly set apart from nonplay reality by special signals and rules. As a result, play is relatively "safe," in that play acts do not have the same consequences that similar acts would have outside of the play space. Researchers have concluded that the primary function of play is to enable us to experiment with different possibilities in our lives, promoting our general flexibility, creativity, and capacity to react well to novel experiences.

These characteristics of play perfectly describe the activity of dreaming as well. Like play, dreaming is autotelic in the sense of being a self-contained, non-goal-oriented activity. The primary function of dreaming is to help us process new information and emotional experiences and to stimulate our capacities for creativity, spontaneity, and self-fulfillment. Dreaming creates a special kind of reality, one that is different from ordinary waking reality, a "safe" environment where we can do many experimental, and sometimes dangerous, things without putting ourselves in real jeopardy (hence our relieved exclamation when we awake, "Thank God it was only a dream!").

The strong similarities between play and dreaming lead us to propose the following thesis: Dreaming is a form of play, the play in which we all engage when our bodies rest at night. To look at dreaming as a kind of play has important implications for how parents should respond to their children's dreams. If a parent walked into a child's room and found the child playing an elaborate game with dolls, dress-up clothes, and toy food, we hope the parent would not say, "Oh, so you're practicing to be a grown-up again," or "That doll is an interesting symbol of your feelings of childhood vulnerability." Rather, the parent would more likely admire the game with gentle, encouraging comments like, "That's so neat!" and "Look how beautiful you've made that!" In the exact same way, parents should welcome the playful creations of their children's dreams with the same open, noninterpretive attitude, admiring and celebrating these imaginative wonders without making disruptive analyses and interpretations of what the parents think the dreams "really mean."

Five-year-old Alice shared the following recurrent dream:

THE BIRTHDAY PARTY
Sometimes I have a dream and it's my birthday party. I get lots of presents. Amy, my friend, gave me a chocolate thing with a white stick.

Alice has cerebral palsy. She can't walk, has only limited use of her arms and hands, and speaks in a thickly slurred voice that is barely intelligible. It would be very easy to dismiss Alice's recurrent birthday party dreams as mere wish-fulfillment, as vain attempts to compensate in private fantasy for the painful handicaps she suffers in waking life. Such an interpretation might have some degree of clinical accuracy, but it would entirely miss the deep enjoyment and happiness that Alice gets from her dreams. Alice is, despite her cerebral palsy, a very bright and cheerful girl, and she gets along remarkably well with the other children at her school (none of whom are disabled). Amy is indeed one of her best friends, who likes playing with Alice regardless of her physical limitations. So rather than being sad symptoms of all the suffering in her life, Alice's dreams are actually evidence of how normal she wants to be, and is. Just like other kids, Alice dreams of playing, having fun, and being with friends; just like other kids, her dreams express a joyful, exuberant creativity. While there are many things Alice can't do because of her cerebral palsy, she can still dream—and the fact that she does so with such innocent, joyful vigor shows how much progress she's already made in overcoming her disabilities.

The capacity to dream is something that all children, no matter what their physical or mental abilities, are blessed with as a natural birthright. With a little encouragement and nurturance from caring adults, this truly magical capacity can grow into a source of lifelong pleasure and enjoyment.

3

A CHILD'S GARDEN OF
COMMON DREAM THEMES

IN EVERY CULTURE AND THROUGHOUT HISTORY, children and adults have had what might be called "universal dreams"—flying, appearing naked in public, being separated from loved ones, finding (or losing) money and jewels, and suffering paralysis. Dreams of teeth falling out, for instance, have been reported by ancient Greeks, medieval Buddhists, indigenous peoples of Africa, Australia, and South America, as well as by modern Americans, Europeans, and Chinese. No matter how much our families, cultures, and conscious personalities differ, all humans share an essential connection in the world of our dreams.

The existence of such universal dream themes has tempted many people to assign fixed meanings to their symbols. And many bookstores sell dream interpretation manuals that catalog the "fixed" meanings of these various images and themes (e.g., dreams of teeth falling out mean x, dreams of falling mean y, etc.). Some of these authors even claim that they'll show you how to interpret your dreams so you could win the lottery!

We call this the "one size fits all" approach to dreams:

you have a dream, you look up its meaning in one of these handy-dandy dream dictionaries, and voilà! Instant interpretation.

Granted, dream dictionaries may provide information and reference points that will spark your own flow of ideas. For example, it may be helpful to learn that other people have viewed dreams of teeth falling out as related to a loss of power, or to a physical or emotional injury, and that fire in dreams has been related to passion or anger.

However, each dream and each dreamer is unique. We believe that every dream must be viewed within the context of the dreamer's personality, culture, and recent life events. Similar dreams may have very different meanings depending on who dreamed them. A dream of being caught in a snowstorm may mean one thing to a person living in Anchorage, Alaska, and quite another to a person living in Miami, Florida, and still something else to a person who has been involved in a serious car accident during a snowstorm. No manual or guidebook could possibly define what such a dream means to all these different people.

The best way to approach the universal dreams of children is to balance a careful focus on the child's current life context with an awareness of what common meanings people have assigned to dreams. In our research, we have found these to be the most frequent types of dreams among children of all ages:

- being threatened by animals or insects
- being chased by monsters
- flying
- falling

- being paralyzed or trapped
- appearing naked in public
- being tested or examined

These typical dreams emerge in reaction to the important events, developments, and transitions that occur at one time or other to all children. By learning how to connect your children's dreams to the key events and experiences, you will understand more fully how your child is attempting to cope with new experiences and challenges.

Being Threatened by Animals

One of the most common types of dreams among children (and among adults) is being threatened by an animal. Almost every parent can expect to hear their children report such dreams at some point. And if you remember a dream from your own childhood, it is likely to be an animal dream.

ANTS

There were ants on my books, and all over my bookcase.

Animal dreams may refer to a recent experience. This dream of Kelly's son Dylan came the night after Kelly had sprayed poison on a trail of ants that had suddenly appeared in the kitchen. Kelly had been very upset about the ants getting into the kitchen, and Dylan had watched as his dad angrily got the poison out of the garage and sprayed it on the ants, killing them all. This incident made a big impression on Dylan, and that night in his dream he imagined what it would be like if the ants came into his special space and invaded the bookshelf in his room. Dylan's dream expressed a very natural fear that those creatures might come after him.

When Kelly heard Dylan describe this dream the next morning, he realized he hadn't even considered how his son might react to witnessing the poisoning of the ants. The dream prompted Kelly to be more sensitive to Dylan's feelings. He reassured Dylan about the "worries" lingering from the dream and explained in simple terms why ants can't come in the house and why he had used the poison.

We call a dream such as Dylan's, which refers directly to something in the child's daily world, a *literal dream:* a plain, straightforward response to a waking-life incident or experience. If a child gets stung by a bee, or menaced by a dog, or scratched by a cat, these animals will very likely appear as directly threatening, dangerous characters in the child's dreams.

More often, though, the animals in children's dreams serve as metaphors—that is, they represent feelings, impressions, or perceptions that are especially hard for children to understand. *Metaphorical dreams* use vivid images to reveal the deepest emotional elements of a child's experiences.

THE WOLF AND THE PIG

In my dream it really sounded like a wolf and a pig were snorting down either side of my head; it sounded like they were going to eat me up.

Eight-year-old Amy's dream of the wolf and the pig is a good example of a metaphorical dream. The images of the

wolf and the pig express the way in which Amy sometimes sees her parents—as large, threatening animals
breathing ominously down either side of her head. Amy's
parents were actually quite loving, and Amy had a very
positive relationship with them. But, as is normal for
almost all children, Amy had ambivalent emotions toward her parents: She loved them deeply, yet she was terribly afraid of their anger. Amy's dream expressed her
fears of the angry side of her parents with the metaphorical images of a wolf and a pig (Amy's father is a
sharp-featured man with a beard, her mother a slightly
overweight woman with a round face). These may not
be especially flattering metaphorical images—sorry, parents!—but they are nevertheless very honest portrayals of
Amy's real feelings.

THE TIGER CHASING MY CAR

*I was driving away from school in a convertible car,
and from behind I saw a huge tiger jump down from
a tree right at me. I tried to drive away faster, but I
knew that the tiger was going to get me.*

Edward's dream of being chased by the tiger is another
example of a metaphorical dream. There are no "real"
tigers lurking around his high school, but the wild adolescent impulses and desires raging within him certainly feel
like savage, man-eating tigers. Edward was sixteen and had
just gotten his driver's license, and he was very proud of
this successful step into the adult world. His dream,
though, metaphorically expresses a deep concern that his
newly won adult status is threatened by the lawless, tiger-

like yearnings that come with being a teenager. This dream made Edward's parents more aware of his adolescent struggles and led to a good, honest discussion about Edward's use of the car. Previous discussions about driving had led to arguments, but using the dream as a basis allowed Edward to assert his need for independence, while at the same time his parents were able to discuss their fears about his driving without igniting a shouting match.

Many of the most common phrases in the daily language of adults use animals as metaphors to describe certain qualities or traits: He's quick as a fox, She's stubborn as a mule, She has an eagle eye, I have a whale of an appetite. However, an adult's view of a particular animal's characteristics may not be the same as a child's. A huge bear in your dreams might make you afraid or anxious, but in your child's dream a huge bear might appear warm, cuddly, and reassuring—an overgrown teddy bear.

To discover what a particular animal means in your child's dreams, we recommend you try the following approach, modified slightly from dream psychologist Gayle Delaney: Tell your child to pretend that you are a visitor from a faraway kingdom, and that you have never before seen a bear (or whatever animal has appeared in your child's dreams). Say to your child, "Could you please describe what this 'bear' animal is like, so I can go back and tell the people of my land about it?"[1]

With an older child or teenager, you might want to explain how this pretend game will help both of you hear more clearly what the dream is trying to say.

Sally, a fourteen-year-old just about to enter high school, kept having this brief but very frightening dream:

CHASED BY THE WHALE

I'm swimming in the huge ocean, all by myself, and suddenly a whale starts chasing after me. I'm very frightened, and then I wake up.

After Sally related her dream, her father described this game to her, and asked her to pretend that she'd never seen a whale before. What, he asked, is this "whale" animal like? How would she describe a whale to a person who had never seen or heard of one before? Sally began by saying that whales are massive, the biggest animals in the world; they eat little fish, swallowing them into their huge stomachs. . . . Suddenly Sally started laughing; she'd realized that the whale's huge stomach reminded her of the high school's vast gymnasium, which she and her junior high classmates had recently visited. Both Sally and her father now understood that the whale of her dream was expressing her fears about starting high school: Sally was feeling like a little fish afraid of being "swallowed up" by the big new school.

This game of pretend is an excellent way of pointing out to your child the metaphorical meaning of a particular dream animal, or of any figure or object in a dream. By trying to describe the animal to "a person from a faraway land," the child will express what he or she feels are the most essential, most important features of the animal. As you hear this description, you will gain valuable insights into the animal's special metaphorical meanings for your child.

Being Attacked by Monsters

Dreams of being attacked by monsters are closely related to animal dreams and are extremely common among children of all ages. For many children, "monster" is a general term they use to represent any number of powerful, frightening forces out in the world or deep within themselves. If children feel capable of managing and relating to those forces, they usually dream about them in the form of animals, but if those forces appear especially vicious and uncontrollable, children will dream about them as monsters.

Sometimes the monsters appear in a guise that parents can readily make sense of. Six-year-old Christina dreamed that "a monster was eating me, it was a dinosaur rex—he ate me!" Christina had, like many children, played with dinosaur toys and watched cartoons about huge dinosaurs battling each other. Her dream frantically mixes together the images of monsters and dinosaurs—especially *Tyrannosaurus rex,* the ravenous king of the dinosaurs—to metaphorically express the very common and very normal childhood fear of being eaten alive. This fear is expressed in many classic fairy tales—"Little Red Riding Hood," "Hansel and Gretel," and "The Three Little Pigs," to name a few. The fear first arises when children discover that humans eat animals, animals eat other animals, and sometimes animals eat humans. Realizing how small they are in this big, voracious world, children are understandably worried that one of those animals or humans might eat them.

Other monstrous creatures parents may find in their children's dreams are vampires, werewolves, boogie men, space aliens, witches, skeletons, and ghosts. By using the "pretend I'm from a far away kingdom" approach, parents can gain further insights into the special fears and concerns their children are expressing through these strange, fearsome monster figures.

In some cases the monsters in dreams have no distinguishing features. They are just monsters. Five-year-old Hannah dreamed this:

MONSTER IN MY HOUSE
A monster ran into my house. He stole everything in the house. He ran away.

Hannah could not describe any details about what the monster in her dream looked like, beyond being male. All she could describe was what the monster did, which was steal absolutely everything in her house.

With such dreams, "monster" is simply the best word children can use to express the terrible forces they see and feel in their dreams. Again, this is a very common childhood fear: Children are painfully aware of how vulnerable and defenseless they are, of how quickly and easily their possessions can be taken away by parents, teachers, or older children.

For this reason, parents should be careful not to push too hard for elaborate details about their children's monster dreams. If your children are willing to discuss what the monster was like, fine; but if they can't describe it, or suddenly don't want to talk about it anymore, that's fine, too. It may be that the "monstrous" fears are so scary that, instead of a lot of talking, what the child needs is a good, warm parental hug.

Occasionally, parents discover in their children's monster dreams a surprisingly familiar face—their own.

Late one night, nine-year-old Eli sleepily walked into the bathroom and was surprised to find his parents engaged in a bitter argument. They both immediately yelled at him to get out. Eli then had the following dream:

MONSTERS IN THE BATHROOM
I was in the downstairs bathroom. A monster was in there, two monsters started fighting with me.

In his dream, Eli expresses very plainly his feelings about this terribly upsetting experience: It was as though two monsters in the bathroom had attacked him. When Eli shared this dream the next morning, his parents realized that their argument was the basis for Eli's monster dream. This knowledge inspired them to pay closer attention to the emotional impact of their occasional fights on Eli, and to reassure him once the fights were over that everything was OK again. It also helped his parents realize that Eli's dreams were a valuable means by which he could communicate emotions he couldn't otherwise express.

Psychologist Denyse Beaudet, who has done research on images of monsters in children's dreams, says that monster dreams tend to fall into three patterns: the child engages in combat with the monster, finds a way to tame it, or (more rarely) is engulfed by it.[2] Beaudet draws on the archetypal psychology of C. G. Jung to argue that, when children dream of monsters, it symbolizes the emergence of a powerful energy within the child's growing psyche: "The monster is a numinous and unknown power, and when the monster appears on the child's path it stimulates the child to become centered and to experience and mobilize his or her own strength." We fully agree with Beaudet when she says that parents should pay especially close attention to images of monsters in their children's dreams, for such images reveal with particular clarity how well a child is doing in the effort to confront the many powerful forces both within the psyche and out in the world.

Flying Dreams

Adults say that their dreams of flying are the most pleasurable, enjoyable dreams they ever experience. This is often true of children as well. Novelist Stephen King says that one of the earliest dreams he can remember is a joyful flying dream:

> FLYING OVER THE FREEWAY
> *I was over the turnpike and I was flying along wearing a pair of pajama bottoms. I didn't have any shirt on. I'm just buzzing along under overpasses—kazipp!—and I'm reminding myself in the dream to stay high enough so that I don't get disemboweled by car antennas sticking up from the cars. That's a fairly mechanistic detail, but when I woke up from this dream my feeling was not fear or loathing but just real exhilaration, pleasure, and happiness.[3]*

Most children experience their flying dreams just like Stephen King did: with a sense of excitement, freedom, joy, and release from the ordinary constraints of waking life. Ten-year-old Jane had this dream:

> FLYING LIKE A BIRD
> *I was a bird, and I was flying through the clouds, with all these other birds around.*

When Jane woke up she could still feel what it was like to be a bird, gliding through the clouds.

When children experience such dreams, parents shouldn't rush to find the dream's "meaning." Rather, they should take some time to join their children in happily lingering with the wondrous feelings of flying, of soaring through the air, of being free and powerful and able to go anywhere one wishes.

Many people in our culture believe that flying dreams are symbolically disguised images of sexuality (yes, it was Freud who said that). Yet, for people in most of the world's cultures, including Australian aborigines, Native Americans, and tribal communities of the Brazilian rain forests, flying dreams are believed to show the soul's ability to leave the body and travel into the realm of the spirits and the great ancestors. When children in these cultures have such dreams, it is often taken as a sign that they may have the talents to become a shaman or tribal healer.

If your children have vivid flying dreams, you really don't need to worry about these differing interpretations (one review of current dream literature has found at least *twenty-four* different interpretations for flying dreams).[4] In our view, all you need to do is encourage your children to simply enjoy these wondrous, magical experiences.

Falling Dreams

What goes up must come down, in dreaming as well as in waking life. The flip side of flying dreams is falling dreams, which tend to be quite scary and upsetting.

Occasionally, a flying dream will be transformed into the

beginnings of a falling dream. Eleven-year-old Kevin dreamed this:

FLYING, AND FALLING, OVER THE PLAYGROUND

I'm flying over the playground, when I swoop down too low and fast, and start falling—I get scared I'm going to crash, and I wake up.

Similarly, eight-year-old Dean had this flying-into-falling dream:

I found some balloons and I untied them from the tree. And I was hanging on to them and I floated into the air. And I couldn't get them down. I was in the sky, and I was scared when I couldn't get down from the balloons.

More often, though, a falling dream involves an abrupt, uncontrolled, downward plunge. For example, seven-year-old Phillip dreamed:

FALLING OFF THE TOWER

I'm on a tower, and I look over the edge, and then I'm falling, down at the water.

Falling dreams may have literal meanings, relating to a frightening experience the child had of falling out of a tree or tumbling off a wall, or perhaps making a rough landing in an airplane. When children suffer such traumatic falls in waking life, their dreams may replay the experience over and over again, as part of the natural recovery process. Parents can help in this process by listening carefully to their children's dreams, empathizing with the frightening emotions, and reminding their children that they're safe now.

In some cases, falling dreams stem from the literal, physical experience of "falling" asleep. The opening scene of *Alice's Adventures in Wonderland* describes this experience perfectly, as the sleepy Alice nods off—and suddenly plummets headlong down a dark, mysterious rabbit hole. The neurophysiological process of shifting from waking to sleeping (with muscles relaxing, heartbeat and respiration slowing, etc.) can easily feel like an abrupt drop or plunge, and children as well as adults frequently have brief, scary falling dreams right at the moment of sleep's onset. Some psychologists have even speculated that falling dreams have their roots in primate evolution: Because our ancestors generally slept in trees, their dreams regularly kept them alert to the danger of falling while asleep on a high tree branch.

When they are metaphorical rather than literal, falling dreams usually refer to experiences in waking life that have made children feel suddenly vulnerable or unsupported. As we might say in a casual conversation, "the ground has disappeared beneath their feet": The children feel that their usual supports are gone, and no one is there to catch them.

When children have falling dreams, the most valuable thing parents can do is offer solid, concrete reassurances that they are really there and will provide their children with the basic support they need. Interpreting the further meanings of such dreams is less important than helping children regain their confidence in the firmness and reliability of their parents' care for them.

Dreams of Being Paralyzed or Trapped

Another very common dream among children is feeling paralyzed, stuck, suffocated, or squeezed so hard that it's impossible to move. Dreams like this may have literal meanings relating either to waking life experiences (being hugged too hard by an adult, being strapped in too tightly by a car seat belt) or to the physical conditions of sleeping. During our nightly experiences of rapid eye movement (REM) sleep, when most dreaming occurs, our bodies actually become immobilized: The brain sends a signal throughout the body that completely relaxes all the muscles to prevent us from physically acting out what we see and experience in our dreams. This natural condition of physical paralysis often enters directly into the dreams of both adults and children.

The metaphorical meanings of paralysis dreams revolve around feelings of weakness and powerlessness. Such dreams commonly appear at times when children feel trapped in a situation they can't change or control.

Andrew was six when his parents got divorced, and for many years his father continued to curse his mother and threaten her with physical violence. The pressure of trying to maintain relations with both parents became more and more intense, and Andrew began having a recurrent nightmare:

> PUSHED DOWN ON THE BED
> *It's the middle of the night and I feel like I'm pushed down on the bed and can't breathe. I can't wake up and I can't stand it.*

It wasn't until he was fourteen that Andrew finally started talking about these horrible paralysis dreams, and he soon found that sharing his dreams with others helped to relieve some of the awful strain he was feeling in his waking life. Once he understood the original basis of his recurring paralysis dreams, Andrew could use each new instance of the dream to alert himself to upsetting situations in his life. This enabled him to ask more comfortably for reassurance from his parents and friends.

In some rare cases, a paralysis-type dream may harken all the way back to the experience of being born and/or to stories children have heard about their mother's birth experiences. Ray had learned that he was a breech baby, and that his mother had a very hard labor with him.[5] Early in his childhood, many years before he really knew what a breech baby was, he started having a recurrent dream:

Trapped in the Tunnel

I'm trapped in this incredibly narrow tunnel. There is just a little bit of room for me to crawl through this place. I have to be very careful as I try to edge my way through this tiny, tiny little opening.

Ray repeatedly had this dream throughout his childhood and adolescence whenever he became caught in a waking life situation that made him feel squeezed or trapped. It's a hotly debated point among dream researchers whether experiences within the womb and during birth can influence later patterns in a person's dreams. But whether or not Ray's dreams of being trapped in a tunnel actually harken back to his being a breech baby, he found the dreams to be a very accurate warning signal of stress and pressure in his life.

Appearing Naked in Public

One of the most distressing universal dreams experienced by both children and adults involves appearing naked in public. Eleven-year-old Denise dreamed this:

> #### NAKED IN THE WINDSTORM
> *A windstorm came and pulled off my clothes and I was embarrassed.*

When Denise shared this dream with her parents she blushed and squirmed with discomfort. The sense of suddenly being naked out in the open, where other people could see her, was so acutely embarrassing that Denise wouldn't say anything more about the dream.

George was seven when he had this dream:

> #### THEY SEE ME POOPING
> *I'm naked, sitting on a small white garbage can near the front door of our house. I'm trying to make a poop, when suddenly all these older kids from school come over. I'm super embarrassed, and I want to get up and run to hide, but then they'll see me. So I just sit there on the white can, trying to keep them from seeing my poop or my private parts.*

Dreams of appearing naked in public may have literal references to experiences of being naked in front of other people, and may perhaps refer all the way back to early childhood experiences of being bathed, having one's diaper changed, and so on. In more metaphorical terms, these dreams usually reflect children's fears that they are going to be "exposed" in front of others—that other people are going to see through their defenses, straight to their most personal feelings and private secrets.

Nakedness in dreams may sometimes symbolize the purity and innocence of a newborn baby. Other times, it may reflect a positive sense of openness to new experiences or a sense of trust. More frequently, dream nudity is a metaphorical shorthand for feelings of painful vulnerability and embarrassing exposure in some area of waking life. If your children have dreams of being naked in public, you shouldn't pressure them into saying more than they want to about the dreams; such pressure could, ironically, replicate the experience of being forced to reveal something private for others to see.

As with children's sexual dreams (to be discussed in chapter five), it is entirely natural for children to be reluctant about discussing such dreams of being naked in public. But even without getting into an elaborate family discussion about these dreams, both parents and children can use them to become more aware of situations in the children's lives where similar feelings of vulnerability and exposure are being generated. Simply knowing that your child is having these feelings can lead everyone to show greater sensitivity at those times (e.g., at school, at a party, at a musical recital or a sporting event) when children are particularly self-conscious and worried about how others are looking at them.

Dreams of Performances, Tests, and Examinations

When children leave home and begin school, they enter a vast new world of rules, schedules, routines, and formal expectations about how they should behave and what they should accomplish. Although teachers and parents try very hard to make this process as smooth and painless as possible, almost every child feels some anxiety about the demands of going to school. Naturally, this anxiety often appears in their dreams, in which children express their emotional reactions to the transition from life in the family to life in a broader social world.

Throughout his first year in nursery school, four-year-old Sam had recurrent dreams of being in his school's classroom. He dreamed of playing with the other children, talking with the teachers, building things with the school's blocks, and many other activities of his daily life at school.

Sam's mother and father were very anxious about how well their son would adjust to his first year of school. When they learned that recurrent dreams are a normal part of a child's efforts to become comfortable in new situations, his parents began encouraging Sam to share with them the stories of his nightly dream visits to his new school. Sam's mother and father soon found that they were learning far more about Sam's feelings about school from discussing his dreams than they were from more direct questions. Hearing his dreams and connecting them with his school experiences eased the worries of Sam's parents and helped them be more sympathetic to their son's struggles.

As children get older, and as their school lessons become more demanding, they often begin to have upsetting dreams about tests and exams. Ten-year-old Jim dreamed this:

I CAN'T DO THE TEST

I am taking a test in school. The bell has gone off but my answers aren't finished yet. I can't write a word, and the time is up, and I'm crying.

Many parents will understand what Jim is feeling, because one of the most common types of dreams among adults is the dream of being back in school and not being prepared for a test or an exam: You're sitting in class, the teacher starts passing out a test, and you realize you haven't studied for it—everyone else is writing away but you have no idea what the answers are, and the clock is ticking away.

Test dreams in adults or children usually arise in response to something in waking life that's made us lose confidence in ourselves. They express our fears that we will fail at something, that we won't be able to meet a difficult challenge. Being unprepared for a test can be a metaphorical expression of any experience of being unprepared or afraid of failing. Dreams exaggerate and distort upcoming challenges. Therefore, test dreams can be a paradoxical indication that the dreamer is going through valuable internal preparation and rehearsal for the upcoming emotional "test" they are facing.

Most adults don't become overly concerned about these dreams, because they know they aren't really in school anymore, and they don't really have to worry about teachers or tests. Children *are* in school, though, and do have to worry about teachers and tests. The pressures of studying complex subjects, competing for grades, and trying to meet the expectations of teachers and parents can easily overwhelm a child. Parents whose children have test dreams like Jim's should reassure them that the dreams don't have to come true; if they study hard, prepare properly, and ask for help when they need it, they will do just fine on their tests.

However, if the dreams continue, parents should carefully evaluate their children's school environment. Is the teacher too strict? Is the class too competitive? Are the children not receiving enough praise when they do well on a test?

Parents should also consider their own role in making their children feel overly anxious about school. All parents naturally want their children to do well in school, but what is intended by parents to be warm encouragement can easily sound to children like high-pressure expectations. Children rarely have the verbal abilities to openly say, "Mom and Dad, I'm doing as well as I can—stop pressuring me!" This is where children's dreams can be so valuable, because in their dreams, children are able to express feelings and emotions that are too difficult for them to articulate directly to their parents. The goal for parents is to learn how to listen to this indirect, but for children less intimidating, form of communication. In this way, children's dreams are truly a magic mirror, reflecting back to parents a true and honest picture of their influence on their children.

Having said all this, we don't want to leave parents with the impression that every child is horribly burdened by the demands of harsh teachers and tyrannical parents. Children are remarkably strong and resilient, and they often find surprisingly creative ways of asserting their independence in the face of all the rules and regulations of school.

An example of this comes from the archive of children's dreams gathered by psychologist Jean Piaget.[6] He tells of six-year-old Gina reporting the following dream:

ALL BY MYSELF

I'm going to school all by myself in the bus. But I miss the bus and walk, all alone. I am late, and the teacher sends me away, and I walk home all by myself.[7]

Gina felt perfectly confident that she could get to school all by herself. Her parents wouldn't let her take the bus or walk to school alone, saying she wasn't old enough yet, but Gina knew that despite their rules she could—and in her dream she proves it. In the happy freedom of her dream she defies all the adults and shows what a big girl she truly is. Teachers and parents may make the rules, but in her dream, Gina gets the last laugh.

Each Child's Dreams Are Unique

Do not fret if your children's dreams and nightmares do not fit the typical dream images we have been describing. There are many variations in the world of dreams, and your child's dream journeys may lead to other gardens than those we have tended here. One child may dream regularly of traveling in foreign lands; another might have frequent dreams of playing with a special toy or stuffed animal; yet another child may have numerous dreams that take place at school or in a particular room in the house.

Parents should be on the lookout for these personal dream themes, because they signal the emergence and flowering of a child's distinctive mode of perceiving, feeling, and behaving in the world. And remember, the task of grasping these meanings can only be performed by you and your child in a process of shared reflection, intuition, and imagination.

4

NIGHTMARE REMEDIES

HELPING YOUR CHILD TAME
THE DEMONS OF THE NIGHT

---

*A monster is chasing me but I am stuck to the floor
with glue and can't get away.* —Jonathan, age seven

*A ghost was trying to crush me. I couldn't breathe
and I woke up.* —Nadia, age fourteen

NIGHTMARES ARE COMPELLING MESSAGES FROM WITHin, warning us to pay attention to situations and people that threaten our emotional security. When events overwhelm us or make us feel out of control, we dream we are falling, paralyzed, or unable to speak. We may find ourselves dreaming of cars going out of control, or planes crashing. Through their disturbing metaphors, these dreams remind us of the need to be on the alert for emotional dangers, to find the brakes, steer the plane, and try to shake off our emotional paralysis.

Most nightmares are a normal part of coping with changes in our lives. They are not necessarily signs of pathology and may, in fact, be positive indications that we are actively coping with a new challenge. For children, this could occur in response to such events as entering school, moving to a new neighborhood, or living through a divorce or remarriage.

Unfortunately, the raw terror that lingers after a nightmare may accentuate a child's insecurity and bring on anxiety for hours or even days afterward. It may even disturb their ability to sleep by inducing insomnia, or fears and phobias about sleeping and dreaming. To help your children restore their capacity to sleep and to harness the healing and creative potential of scary dreams, we must help them break the spell of their nightmares. Guiding your child to "break the spell of a nightmare" includes the following elements:

- Welcome the nightmare with special verbal and physical reassurances to soothe the fear that remains long after a dream of being chased, threatened, or attacked. You might say something like: "That dream must have really worried you. Let's talk about it or draw a picture and then it won't be so scary."
- Reduce the stigma of the nightmare by reminding your child that "all kids and all grown-ups have scary nightmares sometimes. They are very important, but the bad things that happen in dreams don't usually come true."
- Offer to collaborate and invite your child to imagine various fantasy solutions to the threats and dangers posed by the dream: "We can use our imagination and work together to figure out how to keep that monster from hurting you. We might pretend to put him in a cage, wave a magic wand, or make him disappear. Can

you think of other 'pretend' ways to get rid of that monster?"

- Rehearsing one or two strategies that appeal to your child for reducing the power of the monster or threatening element in the dream: "Let's practice pretending to trick the monster into his cage, and we will lock it and throw away the key so he doesn't bother you as much in the future." Or, "Let's turn the phone into a hot line to call your favorite super-hero for rescue services whenever the nightmare villain returns."

By utilizing role-playing and fantasy rehearsals, parents can coach their children to assert their magical powers and tame the frights of the night. New endings for dreams can be created so that falling dreams become floating dreams and chase dreams end with the capture of the villain. When we give our children reassurance and encouragement to explore creative solutions to dream dilemmas, we restore their ability to play with the images in their nightmares rather than feeling threatened or demoralized. These assertiveness skills carry over into future dream confrontations and lead to greater confidence to face waking challenges.

Even very young children can learn to encounter and overcome the threatening creatures of their nightmares. Alan's daughter Sophia mentioned her first dream just before she turned two. She woke from a nap one day and spontaneously said "bird fly outside" while motioning toward the window with her hands. Because Sophia had always been fascinated with the flight and sounds of birds and airplanes, Alan and his wife weren't sure if it was really a dream or just a fantasy. However, a month later, Sophia woke up screaming and sobbing with a bona fide nightmare about spiders.

THE ATTACK OF THE DREAM SPIDER
'Pider on Sophia . . . off Sophia's leg . . . Dad, no more 'pider, please!

While holding Sophia and comforting her, she continued to sob, saying "Sophia scared." Alan reassured her that "Daddy will protect you from spiders." He went on to say, "I am going to teach you how to get those bad spiders away from Sophia." She listened with wide eyes. "When you see those spiders, tell them 'Go away bad spiders. Get out of Sophia's bed and don't come back!'" Alan repeated his antispider anthem three times. Suddenly Sophia smiled a slightly mischievous smile. "Go away 'piders," she said tentatively. She repeated it twice and smiled, waving her hands as if to motion the spiders away. She was significantly calmed, and after a bit of rocking and a short story, she fell back to sleep.

When Sophia woke the next morning, Alan asked, "Did you have any more dreams?" She flashed a playful smile and said, "'Piders!" and laughed. For two more days, she grinned and said "'piders" when she woke. These subsequent dream reports were probably fabricated, judging by the mischievous look on her face. However, within a few days she began to report other dreams, mostly animals, some threatening and some friendly.

Sophia's dream spiders were more terrifying than anything in waking reality. Alan took the dream spiders seriously by talking directly to them and offering Sophia reassurance (both physical and emotional), a concrete strategy for facing the dream creatures and follow-up to reinforce her ability to break the spell of the attacking dream spiders.

The silver lining is that through the often transparent symbolism, children's nightmares shine a spotlight on the issues that are the most upsetting yet unexpressible for your child. To a parent whose ears and heart are open, listening to the most distressing nightmares is like hearing your child's unconscious speaking directly to you, delivering a special call for help.

What Is a Nightmare?

There is no precise point of demarcation where a bad dream becomes a nightmare, although nightmares can be defined as terrifying dreams that awaken us from sleep. The root of the word *nightmare* comes from the Anglo-Saxon word *mare*, meaning demon, and the Sanskrit *mara*, meaning destroyer or to crush. Prior to the twentieth century, most cultures viewed nightmares as an external attack or persecution by supernatural entities such as demons, witches, ghosts of dead relatives, and tribal enemies. These "night-fiends" were often given names and ascribed with deadly characteristics such as the "incubus" or "succubus," who were widely believed to be able to seduce, and then suffocate or crush their nocturnal victims.[1]

For the Ute people of North America, the Baleh Iban of North Borneo, and other tribes, the individual dreamer was helpless without the services of a master shaman, a dream doctor with training in magical rituals designed to exorcise the evil dream spirits by defeating or tricking them. Both ancient and modern descriptions of nightmares include profound helplessness in response to threats to physical or emotional survival and terror of overwhelming intensity. The most common nightmare themes are being chased or attacked, paralyzed, and unable to respond to a mortal threat.[2]

The intensity of the nightmare experience leaves people of all ages with a compelling feeling that the events about which they dreamed *actually* took place—after all, they are often more vivid than waking experiences. The feeling of heightened reality is even more acute and devastating for young children who have not yet reached the point in development where they can fully differentiate dream reality from waking consciousness.

Contemporary psychological theorists generally agree that nightmares are a sensitive gauge of acute psychological distress—an internal warning system alerting us to issues that have overwhelmed our capacity for coping. The painful warning of a nightmare, however, has a hidden benefit. It emphasizes unsolved emotional conflicts and thus orients parents to exactly what kind of attention their child needs. And if we do not pay attention to the messages in our own or our child's nightmare, they will recur, sometimes for years or even a lifetime, until the underlying emotional wounds have been resolved.

Nightmares have many levels of meaning with roots in both the present and the past. Finding the source of your child's nightmare requires going over current life stresses and considering the impact of traumas from the past that could still be influencing dreams years afterward.

Recent events are frequently the stimulus for a nightmare. Sophia, who had always enjoyed eating burritos, had a nightmare at age two and a half about being attacked by an evil tortilla that was trying to smother her. The dream occurred one night after suffering a mild burn from touching a tortilla too soon after it had emerged from the toaster oven. The dream was also influenced by a game that Sophia had recently played with her older sister, when they both pretended to be part of a burrito and wrapped themselves inside a blanket. She wanted to repeat the game because it was both exciting and frightening, like a carnival ride. But the fear of getting trapped in a dark space with no easy exit lingered on and influenced her dream, combining with the memory of being burned—two recent experiences of fear merging in the image of the treacherous, smothering tortilla.

While most nightmares are linked to a recent troubling event, nightmares also flash back to serious upsets from the past. For example, psychiatrist Lenore Terr's research on the Chowchilla, California, kidnap victims revealed that children continued to have related nightmares years after being kidnapped and buried underground in their school bus.[3]

Who Has Nightmares and How Often?

Surveys of adults indicate that many remember only one or two nightmares per year and some rarely have nightmares. On the other hand, those whose lives have been marked by a series of losses, violence, or trauma have more frequent nightmares, brought on by new stresses related to hurts from the past. Other people, who have what nightmare expert Ernest Hartmann calls "thin boundaries," may be troubled by frequent nightmares throughout their lives.

These nightmare-prone people are more emotionally sensitive and more easily wounded by conflicts than others.
They may even be more physically sensitive to noise, light,
or crowds. While people with thin boundaries may be
afflicted with more nightmares, their openness and capacity for empathy make them very effective in the helping
professions as therapists and nurses. They also tend to be
talented in the creative arts, which require openness and
emotional sensitivity.[4]

Children suffer more frequent nightmares than their
parents, and prior to age six, nightmares are especially
common. As soon as your child can speak, he or she may
wake with a one- or two-word tale of a wolf or ghost. There
is even speculation among specialists in child development
that the sleep disturbances of infants in the first year of life
may be wordless nightmares.

Nightmares diminish as children grow older, master
their fears, and gain more control over their world. A long-
term study of 252 children showed that 5 to 10 percent of
seven- and eight-year-olds had nightmares once a week. By
the time children in the study were between ages eleven
and fourteen, disturbing dreams were infrequent, especially for boys.[5]

A good working assumption is that, in children, most
nightmares are reactions to upsetting events and will usually diminish in intensity and frequency as the child and
the family recover from stresses such as a death in the family or the birth of a new family member.

When children feel overwhelmed by events, nightmares
may increase. It is important to keep in mind that often a
stress such as moving to a new neighborhood will be com-
plicated by a chain reaction of other changes. Eight-year-old

Brian and his younger brother Jake were not only moving from the house they had always lived in, they were also changing schools and saying good-bye to all their school friends. After the last day at his old school, Brian's family moved into his friend Colin's house for the summer while Colin's family went on vacation. On the first night of sleeping in his friend's room, Brian had a dreadful nightmare.

In tears, Brian woke and came running into his parents' room, lamenting his bad dream. "I can't stop thinking about the awful smell." Brian's mother, Gina, gave him a sympathetic hug and invited him to sit down and tell her the whole dream. Sobbing slightly, Brian blurted out what he could remember.

POISON GAS

I see my friend Colin and his brother Ross opening the door and going into a dark room like the room I'm staying in. I keep waiting over half an hour but they don't come out. Finally, I decide to go in and check on them. I smell gas and think it might be poison gas. Suddenly I see them lying dead on the floor.

Seeing Brian's distress, Gina wanted to reassure him. "If someone is dead in a dream, does it mean they are really gonna die?" "No, Brian, things that we dream about are important but they don't usually come true when we are awake. Possibly this dream isn't about people dying but about missing your friends after we move." "Yeah, but it was so gross seeing them dead and the gas made me feel like I was gonna get poisoned, too." Gina responded, "That must have been a horrible sight. I would have been scared, too, if I had that dream."

After a moment of pondering, Brian relaxed a bit and said, "That room I'm staying in does smell kinda stinky." He had complained before bed that his friend Colin's collection of old teddy bears smelled bad. Gina agreed, and taking the dream at face value, she suggested that they spray some air freshener before he went back to sleep. As she looked in the cabinets for the freshener, Gina realized that Brian's dream went beyond a simple reaction to the foul smell of the stuffed animals. She realized that she and her husband had been so busy packing and preparing for the move that they hadn't had time to really talk with Brian about his sense of loss and his fears of the unknown.

Brian's morbid nightmare helped his mother understand his emotional needs. As a result of the dream, Gina spent more time talking about the move with Brian and his brother. The family took steps to keep connections with old friends, and visited their new school during the summer to make it more familiar. While in their temporary house, they also moved the smelly bears and deodorized the room.

The poison gas was a response not only to the actual bad smell in the room but also symbolized the dangerous sense of insecurity Brian felt, moving from a familiar home and school and friends to an unfamiliar and unpleasant situation. If death or grief is not a current issue in the dreamer's life, death dreams frequently symbolize loss or painful changes. For Brian, the dark room that swallowed up his friends and killed them expressed his multiple losses as well as fear.

During a period of stress or family crisis, parents should expect more frequent nightmares. Likewise, when children suddenly have more nightmares, they are letting you know they are feeling overwhelmed and insecure. You don't have to interpret or explain the nightmares. Your reassurance and empathy plus some hugs are the first steps toward helping them restore their emotional balance.

How Night Terrors Differ from Nightmares

Night terrors are, for parents, one of the most frightening nocturnal experiences they will come up against. Although your child will forget the experience by morning, you will find it hard to shake the terrified looks, odd rhythmic movements, and blood curdling screams of your child's night terror. The most troubling aspect is the fact that children do not respond to most attempts to calm them, and seem to go through a cycle of ascending panic and apparent physical pain, which gradually subsides almost in spite of our best attempts to be reassuring.

When she was six, Zoe woke up around eleven P.M. shrieking "No! No!" with her eyes open. She was rapidly shaking her arms in unison, apparently trying to ward off some evil spirit. Despite attempts to comfort her, she didn't respond and continued to scream, "No! No! My hands! My hands!" No words or phrases soothed her, only with a firm hug and soft physical caresses did she finally calm down and then fall almost instantly back to sleep with no recall of the incident in the morning.

Night terrors are actually not dreams. They are a form of sleep disorder that primarily afflicts young children. Also called pavor nocturnus, they last about ten minutes and occur within the first third of a night's sleep, often just before or just after you have fallen asleep. Other sleep disorders also occur during this time period, most frequently sleepwalking, sleep-talking, and enuresis or bed-wetting. The first few hours of sleep have fewer dreams and less REM or rapid eye movement sleep. The final hours of sleep have longer and longer REM periods with vivid dreams and fewer night terrors.

The key features in identifying a night terror are that the terror occurs in the first hours of sleep and your child may jump up and move around, scream, cry, whimper, or shout incoherent phrases. Children are often either unresponsive or reject your attempts to soothe them. They undergo a profound physical arousal with agitation, rapid breathing, perspiration, and a racing heartbeat. Only rarely is a dream narrative remembered or recounted at the time of the dream or in the morning. If your child does speak during the episode, he or she might scream of being attacked or threatened with minimal elaboration.

Night terrors are most frequent between ages three and seven, and may be caused in part by immaturities in the developing nervous system. Some researchers hold the view that night terrors are purely physiological, basing their argument on the fact that night terrors are hereditary and many children who suffer from sleep disorders such as sleepwalking and talking also have pronounced night terrors.[6]

Although there is disagreement about whether stress or trauma may be an important factor in triggering night terrors, there are numerous reports of increased pavor nocturnus in a child or even in adults following traumatic events. We believe the reasonable assumption is to assume that night terrors are a physiological reaction to stress, especially when they occur in older children.

Recognizing what a night terror is and when your child

is having one will keep you from panicking. The best medicine for a child with a night terror is a parent's soothing voice and presence. It will take a number of minutes for the episode to run its course, so do not try to restrain your child or forcibly snap him or her out of it. If you can touch or hold your child, a soothing touch or a reassuring hug will help gradually calm the child's anguished screams and frightening, otherworldly behavior, but don't force it.

Recurring Nightmares

Anyone who keeps track of their dreams and nightmares will begin to notice recurring symbols and patterns. Studies of people who have kept dream journals for as long as fifty years have shown that certain animals or houses or people who appear in a person's childhood or teenage dreams will still turn up when their hair is gray.

Your own personal repertoire of nightmare symbols may emerge early in childhood, evolving and transforming throughout your life span. After being stung by a bee when she was three, Annie began to have repetitive dreams of being chased and bitten by bees and other bugs. While her parents initially assumed that the bee sting experience was still bothering her, they began to notice that Annie would get stung in her dreams when other things would upset her: when her mom went on a business trip, when she temporarily lost her favorite doll, just after her brother was born. Her bee sting dreams had become symbolic of events that threatened her security.

Repeating dream patterns brought on by early traumatic events, such as Annie's bee sting dreams, are stimulated later in life by stressful situations. Repeating dream patterns may also be influenced by disturbing images from television and film (no one wants a Freddy Kreuger dream), family fears, cultural stereotypes, myths, and religious beliefs and stories. In chapter eleven, we will tell you how to keep a personal and family glossary of repeating dream symbols. In the meantime, try to recall any of your own repeating symbols and take note of the animals, people, and places in your child's dreams.

What can we learn from recurrent dreams? They are often a warning of lingering psychological conflicts. For example, children of divorce frequently dream that their parents have reunited; abuse survivors are often victims or perpetrators of violence in their dreams; and adopted children intermittently dream of their birth parents.

Conversely, changes within recurring dreams may signal the onset of resolving a psychological impasse. For example, a survivor of child abuse who was making a therapeutic breakthrough in her emotional recovery dreamed of triumphing over a shadowy, hostile figure who had threatened and chased her in innumerable prior nightmares.

In some cases, children spontaneously resolve a recurring nightmare as the formerly distressing situations that caused the nightmares get worked out in real life. Bob, whose tornado dreams were discussed in chapter two, eventually saw remarkable, colorful visions that replaced the terrifying ones in his dreams of twisters. The appearance of the dazzling visions paralleled his increased ability to control his conduct in school and a growing sense of self-sufficiency he developed while his father was overseas and his mother working.

Bob had one other persistent childhood nightmare that

changed decisively with time. Although his father was not inherently cruel and abusive, his stormy personality often led to outbursts of anger that frightened Bob and his sister. After his father's return from military service, Bob began having nightmares about horrific encounters with a ghost-like monster in the basement of his house. These ghost nightmares continued for almost two years, from the age of seven until he was nine.

At first the ghost dreams would leave him shaking in abject terror. As time went on, he would try to stand up to the ghost, but as the following dream indicates, he did not immediately prevail.

SCREAMING AT THE GHOST
IN THE BASEMENT

I was down in the basement in bed sleeping and it was the terror of all terrors. I knew the ghost was around the corner to the right between me and these stairways where you could get back up to the house. I knew if I moved or made the slightest sound the ghost would get me. I couldn't stand the tension so I finally decided I would just yell and let the ghost come out and get me. I sat up in bed and screamed as loud as I could. The ghost came roaring out of its hiding place and jumped all over me and attacked me and I instantly woke up.

Bob woke up feeling simultaneously scared and defiant. Despite the consequences, he was determined to fight back. He later interpreted the threatening ghost as a symbol of his father's angry outbursts.

When his father had returned from overseas, he had not

only interfered with Bob's special relationship with his mother but had been punitive with Bob as he tried to reassert his role as "man of the house." Gradually, as Bob adjusted to his father's presence, he became less intimidated by his father's moods and began to identify with the positive characteristics of his father, especially his father's creativity with tools and building.

Bob's gradually improving relationship with his father was reflected in a breakthrough dream.

DAD HELPS ME FLOAT TO SAFETY

I was at the top of the basement stairs looking down. The stairs disappeared from under me and I was falling and falling into the basement, terrified the ghost would get me when I hit the floor. Just then I saw my dad down there. He turned on this blue light and as soon as he did I floated into the basement and knew that I was safe.

Bob's father, who had been verbally harsh during the months after returning from overseas, had begun to soften and allow Bob to work with him in his workshop, which happened to be in the basement. Providing the blue light symbolized how his father had transformed from a competitor for Bob's mother's love into a positive paternal role model and protector. That positive change in the father/son relationship allowed Bob to work out his recurrent nightmare.

A crucial factor in understanding repetitive dreams is looking at the degree of resolution or mastery in the dream. As children mature emotionally and intellectually, they gain increasing control over their childhood fears and feel more confident in their ability to solve problems and handle situations independently. This gradually increasing sense of control is reflected not only in their waking achievements but in their dream life. Nightmares decrease with age and recurring nightmares show more signs of resolved endings.

Three stages of resolution can be identified in children's nightmares.

- **Threat:** In the dream, a main character is threatened and unable to mount any defense. For example, he or she may be paralyzed while trying to flee the jaws of a hungry ghost imprisoned by aliens.
- **Struggle:** Attempts to confront the nightmare adversary are partially successful in fending off danger. An example would be temporarily escaping a robber with a knife and trying to dial the phone for help.
- **Resolution:** The nightmare enemy, opponent, or oppressor is vanquished and the threatening creatures are put in cages, slain, or held at bay with magic wands or otherwise disarmed.

Everyone agreed that Eric had extraordinary intellectual potential. Talking to him about his interest in science was more like talking to a high school student than an eight-year-old. Yet while his verbal accomplishments were very advanced, his ability to read and write was only adequate. During third grade, he had three repetitive dreams. Each successive dream revealed an increasing mastery of the anger and self-doubts that had limited his academic success.

In the first dream of the series, deadly creatures have invaded the safety of his bed.

MY BED IS MADE OF SCORPIONS

I feel like my bed is made of scorpions, and there are dragons next to my bed scaring me.

For Eric, the usual safety of pillows, covers, and benign stuffed animals have been transformed into a den of danger that might raise the adrenaline of Indiana Jones. This dream does not show a struggle to confront the feared predatory creatures. Nor is there any escape route from this terrifying menagerie of dangerous creatures. In this first stage the dream ends with little or no struggle to overcome a threatening situation or creature.

In the second repetitive dream, there is mortal danger lurking in a dark and frightening place, but the dreamer now has allies and a plan to confront the threat.

FIRE IN THE TUNNEL

I was in this square tunnel and my friends were next to me. Eventually we would have to go into a pit of fire. I wanted to get out of going in there so I kept on going. I never got to the pit of fire before I woke up.

In this dream, Eric wasn't eager to enter the darkness and quench the flames of anger or name and tame the hot formless fear. In fact, he preferred to flee and avoid the danger. Nevertheless, the friends next to him in this dream show elements of a possible metaphoric solution to the danger, and thus suggests a greater degree of resolution.

In the final recurrent dream, Eric's dream has become lucid (he is aware that he is dreaming within the dream).

NINJA VICTORY
I'm with another guy, standing on a brick wall, and there were these giant Komodo dragons that were green with blue spots. I tried to think of a way to get rid of them so I decided to become a ninja guy and I beat them up and killed them.

In the last dream of the series, Eric describes the enemy in rich detail and summons powerful and effective weapons to execute his heroic conquest. The enemy is vanquished. An emotional threat he had been facing was overcome, leaving him with a sense of heroic power and confidence. He preferred talking about this dream and was proud of his relative dragon-slaying prowess.

During the year in which he had these dreams, Eric experienced the stress of adjustment to the birth of a sister. More notably, he made gradual but dramatic breakthroughs in both his academic success with reading and in his social adjustment, finding more friends and having fewer outbursts of anger and sulking at home.

When children or adults keep track of recurring dreams and nightmares, they can often see gradual struggles and eventually partial or total resolution of impasses that crop up within the recurring nightmares. These resolutions usually parallel resolution of the life issues that sparked the nightmares. Conversely, when nightmares persist and do not change or resolve, parents should take time to ponder what events or relationships are causing the child's chronic distress.

Nightmare Remedies

Children do not have to suffer their nightmares in silence, brooding about the lingering feeling of suffocation left by the formless ghost or shuddering at the memory of the razor-sharp teeth of a pack of wolves ripping into their flesh. There are remedies for even the most dreadful, violent nightmares. And every nightmare, no matter how distressing, contains vital information about crucial emotional challenges in a child's life.

Zoe, at age six, had occasional, recurrent nightmares of fire ever since she witnessed the Oakland/Berkeley firestorm[7] when she was two years old. The following dream was one of the worst episodes of this theme.

THE KILLING FIRE

*I was at my school and about six people came and set
fire to the whole school and it burned all the way to
the Golden Gate Bridge and they were going to kill
all the kids and they only chose to save my sister.*

She woke from the dream in the middle of the night, tearfully pleading for hugs and reassurance. She did not feel comfortable or ready to talk about the nightmare at the time or even in the morning before school. Because of her artistic inclination, she was, however, intrigued with the idea of drawing her fire dream that evening, and ended up making a series of sketches with felt-tip markers.

By talking about the elements of her drawing, the bright colors, the architecture of her school, and placement of the Golden Gate Bridge, Zoe was able to begin exploring the dream through the medium of her sketches. This led her to recall some of her earlier fire dreams and to ask a series of questions about the firestorm—how it had started and where she was during the event. She decided she wanted to see the actual site of the fire, which was located quite near some family friends. At the time of the visit, many of the houses had been rebuilt, but she was fascinated by the fact that there were still empty lots and burned-out foundations where homes had once stood.

Like many children her age and older, Zoe did not want to discuss other fears connected to her recent fire dream except to say that she had the dream after watching a violent movie at a friend's house. Although she may have had other worries at the time of the nightmare, her desire not to explore further was respected by her parents. However, her artistic rendition of the dream, her curious questions, and the resulting visit to the fire zone resolved her fire nightmares. Subsequent to her creative exploration of this nightmare, she gradually became more forthcoming in reporting upsetting dreams, even offering ideas about what caused them based on the previous day's events.

Even chronic nightmare sufferers, both adults and children, have found relief from relatively simple treatments and techniques. Vietnam veterans with persistent nightmares have been successfully treated with psychotherapy approaches that focus on resolving both the dreams and the unresolved traumas that caused the dreams to continue.

Barry Krakow and his associates have conducted research with female victims of violence who suffer chronic nightmares. He found that teaching them to create their own fantasy endings brought quick relief of the nightmares and related anxieties. In other treatment approaches, discussing recurring nightmares with a therapist or in a support group brought substantial relief from nightmares that had persisted for years.[8]

It is not clear yet from research whether any one technique is the most effective for relieving the plague of recurring nightmares. In general, what is helpful is sharing the details of a nightmare with a sympathetic, nonjudgmental person, and combining open-ended discussion about the feelings and events in the nightmare with an exploration of the symbols through art, writing, drama, and so on.

The Four R's That Spell Nightmare Relief

There are many potentially beneficial nightmare remedies that parents, family members, and even siblings can use to help a child break the spell of a disturbing nightmare and transform terror into creative breakthroughs. In order to soothe the lingering terror and banish the demons of the night, you must learn the four R's: reassurance, rescripting, rehearsal, and resolution.

Reassurance is the first and most important dimension of remedying children's nightmares. This includes "welcoming the dream," as discussed in chapter one, but with special emphasis on physical and emotional reassurance, which calms children's anxiety and helps them feel safe enough to give details about the nightmare and be open to further exploration.

A nightmare is a traumatic event for children, leaving them with a disturbing residue of anxiety that they cannot shake without help from their parents or a comforting adult. And like survivors of a natural disaster or other trauma, children need to feel that they are not alone. Everyone has nightmares; no one has to bear the pain without help. Reassurance quells the postnightmare jitters and allows you and your child an opportunity to discover both the creative possibilities and the source of what sparked the nightmare that may still be disturbing your child.

Rescripting means inviting and guiding children to imagine changes in the outcome of their dreams by reenacting or rewriting the plot. Even with young children, rescripting is most effective when it is a collaborative process of brainstorming together. The most well-known form of rescripting is creating one or more new endings for a dream using fantasy, drama, and writing.

Rescripting,[9] especially creating a new ending, is like assertiveness training for the imagination. Ominous dream monsters, demons, and werewolves can be tricked and trapped, tamed and leashed, given time-outs, bossed around, and generally made less intimidating. With parental assistance, children with nightmares can be taught to revolt and throw off the yoke of dream oppression through magical means such as fairy dust, a wizard's wand, Star Trek™ "Phasers," special incantations and spells, or other handy tools of the imagination. Very often, developing and rehearsing solutions to dream dilemmas carries over to increased confidence in facing waking conflicts.

During the spring, when nine-year-old Sonya would walk to school with her father, they would see many spiders weaving elaborate webs. Although Sonya's father, a scientist, was eager to teach her about the wonders of nature, Sonya, like her mother, had always been frightened of insects, especially spiders and wasps. In addition, Sonya had become nervous because she had recently begun an after-school program after her longtime baby-sitter suddenly left. Sonya complained that none of her close friends were in the program and that it was boring. On the first night of keeping her Dream Catcher's Journal, she had the following nightmare, which her mother helped her write in her journal.

HUMONGOUS SPIDER

I was walking to school with my dad and on the way we were blocked by a big spider and we both got lots of web on us. The spider was humongous and orange. In the end, I saw a hollowed-out log and tried to go through it like a tunnel, but it had a web on it and I got more web on me and all kinds of black bumps on my head.

After having the dream, Sonya complained that she couldn't get the spider out of her mind. Since Sonya's mother, Terri, was also somewhat phobic about spiders, Terri suggested that they both draw pictures of the spider. Sonya protested, insisting that she wanted to get rid of the spider and make sure she never had that dream again. Having attended a dream workshop for parents, Terri then suggested that they work together to think of new endings for the nightmare. Sonya perked up and suggested that if she had a magic wand, she could create a spider net, "sort of like a butterfly net," to catch the huge spider and throw him far into the woods. Terri asked, "How could you get all the yucky spider webbing off?" Sonya immediately thought of the loofah sponge they keep in the shower and ran to get it and demonstrated by actually putting some liquid soap on the loofah and rubbing her forearm as if dissolving the spider web. Both mother and daughter were feeling empowered and enjoying conquering their fears of spiders together. They decided to take a walk, look for a spider web, and see if their web removal technique worked on the real thing. During an enjoyable jaunt to a nearby park, Terri suggested to Sonya that "scary dreams sometimes tell us something about worries we are having when we are awake." This led to Sonya being able to talk about her discomfort in her new after-school program, and how she missed her baby-sitter. The overall experience helped both mother and daughter reduce their fear of spiders and helped Terri understand Sonya's difficulty adjusting both to the loss of her baby-sitter and her insecurity in the new program. As a result, Terri requested and got permission from her boss to take off an hour early twice a week to pick up Sonya and spend some extra time with her to help her make a better adjustment.

One of the most enjoyable aspects of resolving nightmares is helping your child create his or her own repertoire of "magical tools" for dream assertiveness. These tools are limited only by your imagination and can be inspired by your child's interests, current movies, or television shows; your family's cultural background; books or projects the child is completing for school; and so on. Just as garlic or a crucifix repels a vampire or a silver bullet kills a werewolf, magical tools, such as a special spray for ghosts or an invisible shield for gunmen, can be used to disarm a specific character in a recurring nightmare. Other tools can be of the all-purpose variety, such as the old reliable magic wand, Luke Skywalker's "force" from *Star Wars,* or trusty police tools, like handcuffs or a secure jail cell with the key thrown away!

There are a few areas of caution that should be considered with respect to rescripting. The first is the use of

violence in fantasy solutions to bad dreams. Killing the
nightmare adversary may not be the optimal solution even
in imaginary battles. Ann Sayre Wiseman, author of *Nightmare Help,* warns that suggesting the murder or destruction
of a dream foe may subtly encourage violent solutions to
life problems and reinforce a tendency that children are
already overexposed to through television, movies, news,
and violence in our society. On the other hand, encouraging creative, nonviolent assertion in working out dream
battles may lead to improved and more constructive waking problem-solving skills.

The second caution is about the limits of creating new
endings for nightmares. The popular literature on dreams
has at times left the impression that using fantasy and magical tools to create a new ending implies that the problem
that stimulated the dream has been resolved. This may not
be the case. While impressive results have been obtained
using rescripting to reduce the frequency and intensity of
nightmares, we must remember that nightmares, especially
recurring ones, are messages—even warnings—from within
that we are overwhelmed by a new situation, crisis, or
chronic conflict. When there is a persistent problem in a
child's life, parents may need to go beyond reassurance and
rescripting to find real solutions to the problems that set
off the dream. This leads us to the two final *R*'s—rehearsal
and resolution.

Rehearsal is practicing solutions to a nightmare's various
threats. Going a step beyond the new endings or magical
tools used in rescripting, rehearsal involves repeating the
dream and its solutions in various forms until a sense of
mastery or accomplishment has been achieved. This paral-
lels the stage of psychotherapy called "working through,"

where, for adults, the insights they have gained need to be put to the test—at first in the relationship with their therapist and gradually by practicing new forms of relating with others and experiencing themselves in new ways.

Seven-year-old Kevin had been brought to psychotherapy by his parents because of persistent feelings of sadness and loneliness. Despite being an attractive and bright child, he was extremely sensitive to rejection and always worried whether he was liked by his classmates. Since his family had moved from the Midwest to California, Kevin had been having an especially hard time fitting in. He began to have recurring dreams in which he was always alone. The dreams would usually end with his being excluded while other children engaged in play. At times, he was targeted for rejection, such as in the following nightmare:

ALONE AGAIN

I was with some of the kids from my new school and they were all on this really neat jungle gym with swings that swing way out and a really tall slide. I felt like no one was going to let me on the jungle gym. Then all the kids were swinging up high and flying over a fence leaving me all alone again. The last one was making fun of me and said, "You can't use our swing!"

Kevin was distraught and demoralized by his dream, which reinforced his sense that it was hopeless to make friends in his new school. Kevin's parents were worried and encouraged him to talk about his nightmares in the play therapy session. When he came to the session, Kevin was very willing to give not only the details of the dream but his own version of his history of not being accepted by other children. He seemed especially curious, almost compelled, to work out a solution to his dream. Kevin spent the better part of three weekly therapy sessions trying to rehearse solutions to his dream of being ostracized. He spontaneously grabbed a small X-man figure named Cyclops and developed a scenario where Cyclops was chasing small figurines to try to catch up with them. Repeatedly, he would reach an impasse. Then he began sketching various devices—such as towers, bridges, and Rube Goldberg–like devices—that would get him over the fence to reach the other boys without having to go on the swing. He was encouraged to make up an imaginary dialogue and question his classmates as to why they wouldn't let him play on the structure or swing over the fence with them. Through these fantasy confrontations with the other children, he was finally able to create a scenario wherein he learned that the other children were afraid of someone new and might consider accepting him once they got used to him.

Although Kevin's extensive rehearsal of solutions to his nightmare did not immediately solve his preoccupation with rejection, he did turn a corner in the therapy. He frequently referred back to the sketches he had made and began to make references to one friend in his neighborhood and later a friend he had made at school. After six months, his depression had substantially diminished. He had a small group of friends and had made a solid adjustment to his new school.

Kevin's rehearsal of various solutions to his dreams of rejection gave him confidence to face the issue directly with his peers. The safety of rehearsing ways to assert his needs in private was liberating for Kevin and helped him find concrete solutions to the preoccupation with exclusion that pervaded both his waking and dreaming life.

Resolution is the final stage of alleviating the haunting spell of a nightmare. Discovering the source of the nightmare in your child's life and working toward acknowledging and even correcting the life problem that has caused the nightmares are preliminary steps. Resolution can only come after a child feels secure enough (reassurance) to explore new solutions through art, writing, drama, and discussion (rescripting) and has practiced those solutions (rehearsal) with a parent or adult guide.

If children continue to be curious about what is emerging from explorations of a dream, they can be encouraged to honor their dream by connecting it to a person, situation, or feeling in their life. By keeping in mind the major emotional issues affecting children—the birth of a sibling or starting at a new school—parents can be alerted to the probable sources of a nightmare.

Nine-year-old Evan, a "Star Trek" and science fiction fan, tended to have two recurrent nightmares when his father was away on business trips. In one, his parents would be divorced and his father living far away and rejecting all of Evan's attempts to contact him. The other dream usually involved Evan shouting for his father to help him but having his voice paralyzed.

HELP ME, DAD!

I am on a space ship getting attacked again by the mean aliens. They look like Worf, the Klingon from "Star Trek" and they are throwing sharp spears at me. I can see Dad flying a ship or a plane nearby. I

can see his face but he can't see me. I try to scream to
him for help but my voice is stuck or I am hoarse and
I can't even scream. I wake up just when the spears
are coming at me.

At first, Evan's parents, Don and Jenny, did not associate Evan's nightmares with Don's trips, but gradually it became clear that he not only had nightmares but also increased fear of the dark and more moodiness while his father was away. Since the birth of Evan's twin sisters four years earlier, Evan had become much closer to his father, who helped him with his homework, coached his soccer team, and let Evan come to his office after school to play with the computer games that his father had access to in his job as marketing director for an educational software company. As the company grew, Don was forced to travel more often, sometimes being away two or three days a week.

Because of Evan's enthusiasm for computers, he decided to draw a picture of his nightmare using a computer drawing program and print it on his father's color printer at work. To his picture, he added a special force field that protected him from the Klingon spears. He also came up with the idea of putting a microphone around his neck with a communication device so his dad could hear his calls for help if he had the nightmare again. Evan was so pleased with his drawings that he made four different versions and asked for multiple copies to show his teacher and his friends.

Although the nightmare did not reoccur after Evan starting making his picture, Don and Jenny continued to discuss the nightmares and realized how much Evan was affected by Don's traveling. His emotional attachment to his father had grown much stronger since the birth of the twins, and he was experiencing depression, anxiety, and fears of being abandoned during his father's trips.

Although Don couldn't reduce his travel schedule anytime in the near future, Don and Jenny made a plan to increase Evan's ability to communicate with his father while he was traveling. Because of Evan's precocious interest in computers, they decided that along with occasional phone calls, Don and Evan would send each other e-mail every day.

Although drawing and rescripting his recurring nightmare proved an effective remedy for stopping the dream, addressing his fears of being abandoned and losing the important psychological contact with his father resolved the source of Evan's nightmare.

Through the process of exploring, brainstorming, and rehearsing metaphoric solutions to their children's nightmares, parents begin to feel more secure in linking dream symbols to the current events and relationships in their children's waking world. Nightmares emphasize to parents exactly what is most difficult for their child, and open up possibilities for resolving important emotional challenges.

When to Seek Help for Nightmares

Whereas moderate nightmare activity may be a potentially healthy sign that the unconscious mind is actively coping with stress and change, frequent nightmares indicate unresolved conflicts that are overwhelming your child. When children's nightmares persist, when their content is consistently violent or disturbing, and when the upsetting conflicts in the dreams never seem to change or even achieve partial resolution, it may be time to seek help from a mental health specialist or pediatrician, especially if there is no obvious stress in your child's life. Repetitive nightmares could be caused by a reaction to drugs or a physical condition, so it is advisable to consult a physician to rule out medical causes when nightmares do not appear to have a psychological origin.

A further issue to consider is whether your child may be suffering from a sleep disorder. Many parents confuse sleep disorders like sleepwalking and talking with nightmares, which are more psychological in origin. Sleep disorders may or may not be accompanied by nightmares, and are generally organic in origin. They are surprisingly common, affecting over 15 percent of the U.S. population, with 95 percent of all cases going undiagnosed. The *International Classification of Sleep Disorders*, published in 1990,[10] lists eighty-four conditions that interfere with sleep, including primary snoring, jet lag, restless leg syndrome, narcolepsy, and sleep apnea. Many sleep disorders, such as jet lag, will go away on their own. Others, such as various forms of insomnia, may reduce children's ability to learn, lower their resistance to disease, and increase accident-proneness. Some sleep disorders may even be life-threatening, such as sleep apnea. If you suspect your child has a sleep disorder,[11] speak to your pediatrician to determine if you need to consult a board-certified sleep specialist or have your child evaluated in a sleep center.[12]

The current diagnostic manual of the American Psychiatric Association, the *DSM-IV,* includes "Nightmare Disorder" as an officially recognized affliction of both children and adults. Those who suffer from this disorder have "extremely frightening dreams, usually involving threats to survival, security, or self-esteem" that "generally occur during the second half of the sleep period," and may cause "significant distress or impairment in social, occupational, or other important areas of functioning."

Repetitive nightmares are often accompanied by other symptoms, especially fears of going to sleep, anxieties, or phobias. Increased nightmares can usually be linked to a recognizable stress in the child's life, such as absence or loss of a parent, suffering abuse or violence, marital or custody disputes in the family, and social or academic difficulties at school, such as being teased or having an undiagnosed learning or attention problem.

Nightmares are more often like a vaccine than a poison. A vaccination infects us with a minute dose of a disease that mobilizes our antibodies and makes us more resistant to the virulence of the disease. As distressing as nightmares can be, they offer powerful information about issues that are distressing your child. When children share their nightmares and receive reassurance from their parents, they feel the emotional sting of the dream, but they also begin the process of strengthening their psychological defenses and facing their fears with more resilience. Gradually, a parent's empathic response to their child's nightmares can break the cycle of bad dreams and transform intensely negative experiences into triumphs of assertiveness and collaborative family problem-solving.

5

DREAMS OF GROWING UP

FROM INFANCY THROUGH ADOLESCENCE

IN THIS CHAPTER WE DESCRIBE THE BASIC FEATURES of dreaming through childhood, from infancy to adolescence. As children grow up, their dreams go through a natural process of change, development, and expansion. These transformations are prompted by both internal and external forces—internally by the rapid maturation of children's mental and physical abilities; externally by their ever-widening interactions with others in society. Although every child's dream life is unique, dream researchers have found a number of clear developmental patterns common to the dreams of all children. We have found that the more parents know about these basic features and patterns, the better prepared they are to use dreams effectively as a parenting resource.

The Stages of Dream Development

Thanks to the research of psychologists like Jean Piaget, Erik Erikson, and David Foulkes, we now have a good understanding of the basic stages of development in a child's dream life. Parents should not worry, of course, if their children's dreaming experiences don't "fit" smoothly into these stages. Every child's dreams are unique and should be respected as such.

What follows are simply broad generalizations, based on the best research findings available, about what kinds of dreams parents may expect to hear from their children at any given point in their development.

Ages Three to Five: The dream reports are very brief, with animals, family members, and friends being the most common characters. The dreams are usually set at home or in a homelike setting. There generally isn't much of a plot, nor much emotion or physical activity. The child tends to be a passive observer of the dream's imagery, which tends to revolve around aspects of the child's own bodily states (e.g., hunger, pain, bowel movements, sleep itself).

Ages Six to Ten: The dream reports become longer, with increasing physical action and narrative complexity. Animal characters begin to be replaced by wholly imaginary human characters. The range of settings and interactions expands to include strange and unfamiliar elements. Sex differences become more prominent, with boys frequently dreaming of strange people and untamed animals, while girls usually dream of friendly interactions and happy outcomes. The most common feelings children of this age report in their dreams are happiness, friendliness, and a sense of belonging, although the overall range of feelings expressed in the dreams of children this age remains much narrower than those expressed in the dreams of adults.

Ages Eleven to Eighteen: The dreams now approach adult averages in terms of length, coherence, and complexity. The emotions of fear and anger become more common, with higher numbers of unknown characters and aggressive interactions. Images pertaining to the physical transformations of puberty are, of course, very common, with increasing dream references to sexuality, menstruation, and changes to the adolescent's body. At the same time, dreams at this age also become more abstract, speculative, and imaginatively diverse as the child's mind develops the ability to think about possibilities beyond the constraints of objective reality.

The Dawn of Dreaming

When do children first start dreaming? Although psychologists have debated this question for decades, no one has come up with a definitive answer. In the 1950s, sleep laboratory researchers discovered that every human experiences four to six periods of rapid eye movement (REM) sleep several times each night. During REM sleep, the heartbeat increases, breathing quickens, and the brain becomes extremely active (in some ways even more active than when we're awake). When subjects in the sleep lab are awakened during non-REM sleep they usually do not recall any dreams, or simply describe random, somewhat disorganized thoughts about ordinary daily life. But when subjects are awakened during or immediately after REM sleep, they generally report just having had a dream with vivid imagery, several different characters, and strong emotional content. Based on this evidence, psychologists have concluded that REM sleep is the time when most of our dreaming occurs.

Of greater interest to parents, researchers have also found that infants and very young children experience much more REM sleep than adults. An adult human spends 20–25 percent of an average night's sleep in REM —that is, about one and a half to two hours of REM per night. But infants are in REM in more than 50 percent of their total sleep time. Massive amounts of REM sleep have even been detected in fetuses sleeping within the womb!

Does this mean that at birth we are dreaming almost continuously, and that as we grow older we gradually lose our abilities to dream? Did the poet William Wordsworth truly anticipate the findings of psychological research when he wrote that we are born into this world "trailing clouds of glory," and that "our birth is but a sleep and a forgetting"?

A six-week-old boy named Jimmy was napping in his nursery one afternoon when he suddenly started making loud and very strange noises. His mother and grandmother both rushed into the nursery to check on him, and were surprised to find that Jimmy was giggling in his sleep— laughing hysterically, just cracking himself up. His mother knew that Jimmy had not yet laughed while awake, but here he was, deeply asleep, merrily giggling away. His mother was relieved that at least Jimmy hadn't thrown up or fallen out of his crib, and she thought nothing more of his sleepy giggling. But then, a week later, she heard Jimmy laugh aloud while awake for the first time, in exactly the same way he had during that nap.

One of the widely recognized psychological functions of dreaming is to prepare us for future tasks, challenges, and experiences. Seen in this light, little Jimmy's naptime laughter seems to have been practice for the real thing—in his sleep, in his dreams, he was testing this newfound ability, trying it out, preparing to use it in waking life. For a six-week-old baby, the ability to laugh is a major developmental accomplishment, opening up a whole new realm of emotional expression and social interaction. The fact that Jimmy laughed first in his sleep, and then a few days later in his waking life, suggests that he was, like the rest of us, dreaming about how to prepare for the challenges lying just ahead.

Another intriguing observation about the dreams of young children comes from the founder of psychoanalysis, Sigmund Freud.[1] When his youngest daughter, Anna (who later became a famous psychoanalyst herself), was nineteen months old, she had an attack of vomiting one morning. She was prevented from eating anything else that day, and during the night her parents heard her calling out excitedly in her sleep, "Anna Fweud, stwawbewwies, wild stwawbewwies, omblet, pudden!" Freud said that it appears his toddler daughter was dreaming this delightful menu of her favorite foods because she had been denied them while awake—just as adults regularly dream of things they greatly desire but which they have been unable to gain in their waking lives.

Dreaming in the Preschool Years

Children first tell us about their dreams around the ages of two to three, when their verbal skills have developed sufficiently to communicate the strange experiences they have had while sleeping. Dreams reported by preschool children tend to be very short and static, with little explicit emotional content. Animals, friends, and family members are the most common characters, and the child tends to be a passive observer of what happens in the dream, as the following examples indicate.

> *I had a dream of Timmy, he was a hockey goalie.*
> *—Simon, age four*

> *Batman rode on a horse. —Martin, age three*

> *One alligator comes and I'm very nice and he doesn't bite. —Mikhaela, age four*

> *I had a dream about lightning, the rain comes down from the sky and I saw lightning. —Logan, age four*

> *I had a nice dream. A mouse was in it. It squealed.*
> *—Allie, age three*

Parents should not be fooled by the brevity of these early dreams. The first dreams that children consciously remember often evoke a deep sense of wonder and amazement.

Kelly's son Dylan woke up from his nap one afternoon and looked around his bedroom, with a look of utter perplexity on his face.

"What's wrong?" Kelly asked.

"My school, it was right over *there*," Dylan answered slowly, pointing to a spot on the other side of his room. "But now . . ."

Kelly sat down on the bed next to Dylan. "But now it's gone, and it's just your room again?"

"Yeah," Dylan said, shaking his head. "That was so weird. It was really *there,* and Merlin [one of Dylan's best friends] was there, too. Was that a dream?"

"I think so," Kelly said. "That's the way a lot of dreams are—they feel very real while you're having them, but then you wake up and you're back in your bed. They're both 'real' and 'unreal' at the same time."

Dylan thought about that for a moment. "So dreams are kind of like stories?" he finally asked. "Kind of real but kind of not?"

"That's right, dreams are like stories we tell ourselves when we're sleeping."

"I gotta tell Merlin about this!" Dylan said with sudden enthusiasm. "He's going to think it's really *cool!*"

Although the content of Dylan's dream was brief and unremarkable—being at his nursery school—the feelings it generated in him were very strong, and he was eager to explore them and understand where they came from. Parents should always be aware that dreams which sound short and static to them may be incredibly fascinating and meaningful experiences for their children.

As has already been mentioned in the chapter on nightmares, the dreams of preschoolers are often terribly frightening. Young children are painfully aware of how small and weak they are in a world filled with tall grown-ups, complex machines, and ferocious animals. Nightmares are a very natural, very normal response to these feelings of vulnerability. Through their nightmares young children work at developing the inner resources necessary to fend off the various threats and dangers that frighten them in waking life. Paradoxical as it may sound, frightening dreams are often a sign of healthy adaptation for children. So to repeat, parents should not worry too much if their children have occasional nightmares. Like bruised shins and scraped elbows, scary dreams are just another part of growing up and learning how to get around in the world.

Parents, siblings, and friends frequently appear as characters in the dreams of preschool children. Dreaming so frequently about these familiar people helps to strengthen young children's emerging abilities to form interpersonal relationships—a key element in the healthy development of any child. It's as if the children were repeating to themselves, "These are the people I know, these are the people I like best and trust most, if I ever need help I can rely on them." The dream images of parents, siblings, and friends reassure children that even in the dark solitude of sleep their closest, most trustworthy companions are still with them.

Occasionally, children's dreams of familiar people will portray them in a more negative form. Sometimes, in a dream, parents and siblings are totally transformed into images of wild animals or even terrible monsters. Eli's dream, described in chapter three, is a good example of this. After witnessing a bitter fight between his parents, Eli dreamed "I was in the downstairs bathroom. A monster was in there, two monsters started fighting with me." As much as Eli loved and trusted his parents, the experience of seeing them fight made him feel there was also something "monstrous" about them, something fearful and threatening. Like Eli, most children have ambivalent feelings toward their parents, both loving them and to some extent fearing them. Because children's dreams are so emotionally honest, they sometimes portray parents as nurturing caregivers, and other times imagine them as dangerous monsters.

For some young children, their most trustworthy companions in both waking and dreaming life are not people but toys, playthings, and imaginary friends. Liam was two and a half years old when he learned that his mother was pregnant with her second child. A few weeks later Liam created an imaginary friend, "baby Gingie," who was a baby dinosaur that Liam said he had hatched from an egg. For the next several months baby Gingie was a major figure in Liam's life, joining him at mealtime at the kitchen table, riding along with him in the car, and cuddling into bed with him at night. Besides providing Liam with the reliable daytime companionship his pregnant mother could not provide, baby Gingie also helped defend and protect him in his dreams. Liam reported several dreams in which monsters were chasing him; whenever the monsters came, he and baby Gingie would "bang them down." In these dreams, Liam would grow a horn just like baby Gingie's, and the two of them would successfully fight off the threatening creatures. Although baby Gingie was only "imaginary," he provided very real friendship at a time when Liam needed it most.

The biggest developmental challenge children face at this age is leaving home and starting school. For some children, the transition begins relatively early, with day care or nursery school; for other children it comes later, with kindergarten and grade school. But whenever it comes, the transition always brings with it a lively mix of nervousness, excitement, and uncertainty. These anxious feelings about leaving home and starting school naturally appear in children's dreams, and if parents listen carefully to these dreams they can gain insights that will enable them to help their children adjust better to their new life in school. Four-year-old Sam, whose recurrent dreams of being at school were described in chapter three, is a good example of how a child's dreams can become a valuable source of conversation between him and his parents about both of their feelings toward starting school. As Sam would wake up each morning and eagerly describe another dream about his new nursery school, his mother gradually realized that by sharing his dreams with her, Sam was preparing himself for a new day's worth of experiences, challenges, and adventures.

While dreaming frequently about school is a normal occurrence for any child leaving home for the first time, sometimes a child's dreams do signal a real problem at school that needs parental attention. When three-year-old Hank started attending nursery school, he was very excited at the opportunity to play with so many other children. But one morning an older, more aggressive boy fought with Hank for a toy; when Hank resisted, the boy bit him on the cheek, breaking the skin. The teachers reassured Hank's parents that this was an isolated incident and that nothing like it would happen again. But these reassurances were little help to Hank, who began dreaming repeatedly of struggling against animals with sharp teeth who threatened to bite him. These are some of his dreams:

THE SHARK TRIES TO BITE ME

There was a shark. He was bad. He had some teeth and a tongue and he tried to bite me and I told him to stop and if he bites me I will bite him back.

The Mouse Bit Me

There was a mouse in my bed. He bit me. I chased him out of my bedroom. He's gone.

My New, Sharper Teeth

My old teeth are gone. I gave them to another old guy. A white donkey gave me some new, sharper teeth.

Sharing his dreams with his parents enabled Hank to express the emotional complex of fear, vulnerability, and anger that had been so deeply troubling him. In his first dream the image of the "bad shark" directly reflects Hank's frightening interactions with the older boy at school. The second dream, of a mouse coming into his bed to bite him, seems to indicate Hank's sense of vulnerability, how scared and threatened he felt even in the normally safe space of his bedroom. However, this second dream also points to an emerging ability in Hank to confront his fears and "chase them away." His third dream continues that theme of trying to find the inner power and strength to defend himself against being bitten again.

Hearing their son's recurrent nightmares of biting helped Hank's parents understand how terribly frightened he was by the older boy's aggression at school, and how hard Hank was trying to find a way to protect himself from further threats. His mother and father kept a close watch on the situation, and when the older boy bit Hank again a couple of weeks later, they did not hesitate to confront the teachers and insist that the older boy be prevented from attacking their son again.

Dreaming in the Grade School Years

As children get older, their dreams gradually become longer, more dynamic, and more complex. These changes reflect their increasing cognitive skills, their growing sense of personal autonomy, and the widening of their social world.

In the dreams of six- to ten-year-olds, significant differences between the sexes begin to emerge. Psychologist David Foulkes, who performed the pioneering study in 1982 on the dreams of children in this age group, found that girls start having dreams with more known female friends and adults, and with fewer unfavorable outcomes and incidents of aggression.[2] Boys in this age group dream more often of strangers, untamed animals, and outdoor settings, and have more incidents of physical activity. Here are some of the dreams reported by two of the children in Foulkes's study:

SKIING AND SWIMMING
I went skiing at a place and I broke my leg. I went again and nothing happened, so I kept going, and then I broke it again so I finally quit and I started to take up another sport, swimming. —Dean, age eight

THE FOREST THAT WOULDN'T BURN
Some friends and I were tree planters and we went up to this place and we planted a tree. And the next day we came back and the tree was already grown. So we planted more and they all grew and there was a forest

fire and they wouldn't burn down. So we made forests out of them, and then some men were chopping them down for firewood and when they chopped them down the fire wouldn't work. So they told it to the state police and the mayor said that the boys planted those trees and they won't burn. —Dean, age eight

PLAYING IN OUR HOUSE

There was a little boy and two girls and they lived in our house. And the little boy wanted to play, and so he came out into the kitchen, and he asked the mother if he could play with his blocks in his room. And so he went out and played and the two girls stayed in the kitchen, sitting at the table, eating. —Emily, age ten

MY TEACHER AT SCHOOL

I was in school and the teacher was up at the board talking and showing us something, writing on the board. We have some science projects to do at school and she was telling us we had to hand in one project and she was talking about how we'd have to do it. —Emily, age ten

The study that Foulkes conducted was based on dreams reported in his sleep laboratory: He would awaken the children sleeping in his lab several times during the night and ask them to describe whatever was going through their minds. This highly artificial setting naturally affected the kinds of dreams the children experienced and reported to Dr. Foulkes, and we must disagree with his study's conclusion that children's dreams are basically tame, unexciting mental representations of the ordinary events in the children's lives. However, we believe that many of the dream reports he received, such as those quoted above from Dean and Emily, do give valuable insights into such questions as how the dreams of boys and girls differ.

We will discuss in more detail the impact of sex stereotypes on children's dreams in chapter nine. For the moment, we simply want to note that parents should not be surprised to see the appearance of sex differences in the dreams of their grade school children. Living as we do in a world where boys and girls are taught to think, feel, dress, and behave in very different ways, it is perfectly natural for children to explore in their dreams the relationship between these stereotypes and their own emerging sense of personal identity. In chapter ten we will offer some suggestions on what parents can do to help their children resist the worst influences of our society's views on proper sex roles.

Another new development in the dreams of grade school children is the appearance of anxieties about time, tests, clothing, and other forms of social pressure and expectation. Parents are often surprised to hear their seven- and eight-year-old children complaining of the same typical anxiety dreams that plague adults—dreams of being late and rushing frantically after a departing bus or airplane, dreams of being unprepared for a test, dreams of being naked or inappropriately dressed in public, and so forth. While children at this age greatly enjoy their newly won social abilities, they also worry terribly that they will fail to meet the demanding expectations of the grown-up world.

Generally speaking, parents should not become overly concerned if their children occasionally have such anxiety dreams. However, if a child begins having repetitive dreams of being late or of failing a test, the parents may want to take some action to help relieve the pressures on their child. Often, simply hearing a parent say it's OK to get less than a perfect score on a test can be a huge, welcome relief to a grade school child who is valiantly striving to do what he or she thinks parents, teachers, and the rest of society expects.

A major developmental task for children in the six- to ten-year-old range is learning to control their inner impulses and adapt themselves to the demands of external reality. While preschool children still live in a world of fluid boundaries between fantasy and reality, grade school children are expected to begin distinguishing what they wish and desire from what is realistic and socially proper. As with any developmental transition, this one brings with it exciting gains and saddening losses.

Grade school children are filled with curiosity about how the adult world works; they love learning new skills, gaining new competencies, and becoming capable, self-possessed members of the community. However, children at this age are also mourning the loss of their early child-hood, when everything was alive with magic, when fantasy reigned supreme, when their parents could easily pick them up and cuddle them whenever they cried. The deep emotional tension between these feelings of anticipation and grief explains why the moods of grade school children so quickly swing from swaggering self-confidence to baby-ish pouting and back again.

Although nothing but time can make this painful ten-sion go away (and even time doesn't eliminate it com-pletely—how many of us adults still struggle with the conflict between inner fantasies and outer realities?), we do have a suggestion for parents who want to ease the emotional strains children often feel at this age. Sharing dreams with grade school children can be a valuable way of helping them strike a healthy balance between their exciting entrance into adult reality and their saddening loss of "babyish" pleasures. Parents can reassure their children that their dreams are a living connection to those deeply cherished wishes and desires from early childhood, and that becoming more of a "grown-up" does not mean rejecting or forgetting those parts of themselves. At the same time, frequent dream-sharing can help them further strengthen their emerging capacities for objectivity and self-control: The more grade school children discuss, examine, and think about their dreams, the more confident they become that they can understand and master their internal urges.

Teen Dreams

Adolescence is, of course, a time of tremendous change and upheaval in a child's life. The relatively stable personal identity a child has developed through the grade school years is suddenly shaken by the radical physical and hormonal changes occurring in his or her body. In addition to this tumultuous process of sexual maturation, adolescents must also learn how to navigate through the sometimes vicious world of peer relations to find friendship and romantic intimacy. And if that weren't enough, adolescents face the additional developmental task of trying to become competent in an expanded set of roles in the adult world (e.g., learning how to drive a car, how to work at a job, how to budget money).

All of these difficult yet exciting transformations are

reflected in the dream lives of adolescents. In fact, their dreams are a perfect mirror of their "betwixt and between" status in the world: Like adults, adolescents have dreams with lengthy narratives and complex visual-spatial imagery; but like preschoolers, adolescents have remarkably frequent nightmares. In both their waking and dreaming lives, adolescents struggle with their experience of being children and adults at the same time.

One new type of dream that all adolescents experience at one time or other is the explicitly sexual or erotic dream. For most adolescents, sexual dreams occur before any actual sexual encounter (meaning that parents should *not* automatically assume that an adolescent who has a sexual dream has in fact been sexually active). Just like six-week-old Jimmy's dream of laughing, which served as a kind of "trial run" for laughing in waking life, so the sexual dreams of adolescents give them a safe, private opportunity to experience and explore this powerful new realm of physical and emotional sensation.

When Bob, the boy whose colorful tornado dreams and terrifying ghost nightmares were discussed in earlier chapters, was just entering puberty, he had a dream that both expressed and stimulated his deep curiosity about sexuality. Bob and a girl at his school had decided to be boyfriend and girlfriend together. Bob was thrilled, but also scared—he didn't really know what girls were like or how to behave toward them. Then one night he had this dream:

SEEING MY GIRLFRIEND'S PRIVATE PARTS
I'm with my girlfriend, and we're being very romantic with each other, hugging and kissing and things like that, and then somehow she took off her clothes,

and I looked at the area of her private parts—and
what I see are patterns of spirals, squares, and circles
of rainbow color, and I'm fascinated and excited by
how beautiful they are.

In chapter two we saw how Bob's nightmares of ominous tornadoes were symbolically expressing the worries he felt about his new school and his unsettled home life, and we saw how Bob could cope better with his worries once he learned in his dreams to recognize and appreciate the beautiful rainbow colors in those tornadoes. Here, later in his childhood, Bob overcomes a new set of anxieties with the help of a strikingly similar kind of dream revelation. This dream about his girlfriend reassures Bob that even though he doesn't really know very much about sexuality or about women's bodies yet, he doesn't have to be scared; on the contrary, Bob's budding sexual yearnings are given powerful encouragement by his dream. Just as his tornado dreams led Bob to understand that confronting his fears could open up new possibilities in his world, so this dream showed him that this new realm of sexual intimacy and romance is filled with mysterious but beautiful wonders.

Generally speaking, parents are not likely to hear about an adolescent's first erotic dreams—these dreams are so private that adolescents rarely share them with anyone, especially their parents! But parents can still help their children with these dreams, simply by reassuring them that sexually arousing dreams are natural, normal, and nothing to be ashamed or embarrassed about. Particularly for adolescent boys, whose nocturnal emissions or "wet dreams" may be painful reminders of past experiences with bedwetting, such parental reassurances can be very helpful.

For adolescent girls, the onset of menstruation usually brings with it a series of dreams that express their feelings about this amazing new physical process. Some of these dreams may be joyful, reflecting a girl's exuberant discovery that now she can have a baby. Some of them may be scary, indicating a girl's fear that menstruation is somehow shameful or disgusting. As with erotic dreams, menstruation dreams are not likely to be shared with parents. Still, parents can tell their daughters that dreams about menstruation are absolutely normal, and that such dreams can be a source of deeper understanding for them about what it means to become a woman, capable of conceiving and bearing a child.

The most common contents of adolescent dreams revolve around interactions with friends, siblings, parents, and teachers. In these dreams, adolescents reflect on their waking-life efforts to form various kinds of mature personal relationships. Because these waking-life efforts are so often filled with tension and conflict, the dreams of adolescents frequently have an anxious, frightening quality.

Other common adolescent dreams involve a struggle with some new duty or responsibility in the adult world. Alvin was a seventeen-year-old who had been working at a record store for several months before it went out of business; the store owner said he thought he could get Alvin another job at a different record store, but he wasn't sure. While waiting for news from his former boss, Alvin had the following dream:

I FALL ASLEEP AT WORK
I was working in a bookstore, but it was more like a record store. I was new there and at first was doing

well. Then I was tired and I was sleeping at work. I
also was going outside talking to people. I was also
lying down on the sidewalk. I got worried that I'd get
fired. I decided I'd have to try harder.

Although Alvin didn't particularly like working, he had
always taken his job at the record store very seriously; if
he got sick, he might stay home from school, but he never
missed going in for his shift at the store. Alvin's dream
reflects the whole range of emotions he felt toward work:
pride at doing well, exhaustion at the effort working
required, fear of failing and getting fired, determination
to try harder. As he anxiously waited to hear about the
new job (which he did get), Alvin's dream expressed the
ambivalent meaning of work in his young life. Becoming
a reliable, hard-working employee is a basic feature of
adult identity in our society, and like all adolescents,
Alvin was struggling to meet the challenges of growing
into that role.

The final example we want to discuss in this section is
that of Dana, a thirteen-year-old whose dreams following
the suicide of rock star Kurt Cobain summarize in many
ways the swirling complexity of hopes, fears, and conflicts
found in the dreams of adolescents.

KURT COBAIN
IS MY BEST FRIEND

I was playing under my house. And all of a sudden
Kurt Cobain appeared. We had so much fun together.
He was my best friend. We talked and just hung out
together. He understood me. We went into the back-
yard and talked some more.

ASKING KURT NOT TO KILL HIMSELF

I was at some sort of concert or movie set. I was hanging out with Kurt Cobain. I was the only one he would let in his trailer (besides his daughter, Frances, and his wife, Courtney). We would walk past people and they were so jealous of me. I hung on to Kurt. I guess I was kind of being obnoxious. But Kurt didn't care because we were friends. Once we sat down in his trailer we started talking. I said to him, "Kurt, in another life you killed yourself." He got this really serious look on his face. "You left Frances and Courtney, and all your fans, and me. You've got to get help now, or you'll kill yourself in this lifetime, too." Kurt nodded his head. I knew he would get help. I felt so happy—when I woke up, I wished that encounter had really happened.

TAKING CARE OF FRANCES

I was taking care of Frances Bean Cobain. She was the sweetest thing. I hugged her and played with her. All too soon her mom came to pick her up. Courtney looked so motherly. She was dressed in black stretch pants and a black sweatshirt, and she had a diaper bag. Courtney said to me, "Where is her ice cream?" Frances's face was covered in ice cream. I go to the spice cabinet and get out an ice cream. I give Frances the ice cream, and they leave.

Like millions of other teenagers, Dana was shocked and terribly depressed when Kurt Cobain, the leader of the rock group Nirvana, suddenly committed suicide in April 1995. To his fans, Cobain was a voice for the frustrations so many of them were feeling, growing up in families crumbling from divorce and abuse, looking at a society with few job prospects, and watching the chasm widen between the haves and have-nots. By killing himself so violently (putting a shotgun to his head), Cobain seemed to confirm that despairing sense of hopelessness shared by his fans.

Dana's dreams express her emotional struggles to make sense of Cobain's suicide. Her first dream emphasizes her sense of intimacy and closeness with him; as she plays "under the house," away from the prying eyes of her parents and siblings, Kurt is with her. Dana feels a kinship with his "outsider" status, and this almost spiritual connection between them is tremendously reassuring to her—she isn't alone in the world, there's someone else who knows what she's feeling. Dana's second dream starts in a similar vein, with her enjoying a special intimacy with Kurt. But now she feels strong enough to challenge him, and to question his decision to kill himself. In the process of telling Kurt how much his suicide hurt his child, his wife, and his fans, Dana reaffirms for herself the supreme value of human relationships: No matter how hopeless a person feels, no matter how dark and empty the future may seem, you have to remember the people who care for you. In her third dream, Dana follows through on this ideal, as she takes care of Kurt's two-year-old daughter, Frances Bean. Kurt may be gone forever—this dream finally acknowledges that sad fact—but his daughter is still alive, and still needs attention and care. Dana discovers through these three dreams that she has the ability to provide that kind of nurturance, that despite the anxieties she and so many adolescents feel about the future, she can find real hope and fulfillment in caring for others.

Childhood's End

When adolescents finally leave their parents' home, either to go away to college or to move into their own home, their dreams frequently harken back to the fearful nightmares of preschoolers. Sadness at leaving one's parents behind, excitement at the broad new horizons ahead, and anxiety about one's abilities to make it alone all combine to generate particularly vivid dreams during this final stage of childhood. Just before eighteen-year-old Edward was to leave for college, on the other side of the country from his hometown, he had this dream:

IT'S WORLD WAR III

I'm standing on a hill overlooking my town. It's like it's World War III, and everything is about to be blown up by nuclear bombs. I think that maybe I should try to find a market and get some food so I can survive.

This dream indicated that, for Edward, leaving home to go away to college felt like the "end of the world," like the nuclear holocaust that would happen if World War III ever broke out. To survive in the postholocaust world, far away from his family and his hometown, Edward would have to start taking care of himself. Trying to find food in the dream is an apt symbol for his need to become more responsible for his physical and emotional sustenance. Looking for a market ties in with the need for "food," and also points Edward toward one of the primary goals of college life—preparing for a career in the adult world, and developing skills that will enable him to get employment in the job "market."

As is true with so many dreams, Edward's portrayal of going away to college as World War III had an extremely dramatic, exaggerated quality. In this case, the exaggeration was so outrageous that it actually made Edward laugh: The dream both mirrored his feelings and mischievously poked a little fun at them. Reflecting on his dream helped Edward to ease his worries and to develop a more realistic perspective on what going to college meant to him.

Parents can expect similar "childhood's end" dreams at any point in a child's life when he or she is making a developmental separation from the family and learning how to feel comfortable as an autonomous person. While the dreams of an adolescent leaving home for college may be particularly vivid illustrations of this process, younger children also experience dreams that reveal their sometimes rocky growth toward independence. When Kelly's four-year-old daughter Maya entered her second year of nursery school, she suddenly found herself a "big kid"—her older brother Dylan had left the school to start kindergarten, and now Maya began enjoying the new feelings of maturity, competence, and self-esteem that came with being a veteran at the school and not having her brother around to overshadow her. One night Maya had this dream:

I WANT TO GO IN BONNIE'S CAR

I'm going to Lily's fourth birthday party, and I want to go in Bonnie's car; I don't want to go with Mommy and Dylan in their car, because there are too many boys in that car.

Bonnie is one of Maya's favorite teachers at her nursery school (and, as it happens, the teacher who most physically resembles Maya's mother). Lily is a friend from school who, like Maya, had just turned four. In the dream, Maya asserts her newfound independence by choosing to go to the birthday party with Bonnie rather than with Mommy and Dylan; she wants to interact with her four-year-old friends as a peer, as another "big kid," and not as someone's youngest child or little sister. Maya is not rejecting her family entirely in this dream (as indicated by the image of Bonnie, who is the most "mommylike" teacher at the school). Rather, Maya is expressing how important it is for her to preserve the relative sense of independence and autonomy she has gained in her second year of nursery school. Hearing Maya describe the dream, and her very strong feelings about whose car she wants to go to the party in, made Kelly and his wife more aware of just how big a kid their daughter was becoming.

Dreams and Emotional Communication

The theories of most developmental psychologists divide a child's growth into physical, emotional, cognitive, and social aspects. But parents know from personal experience that these different elements of their children's growth are all interconnected. In the busy activities of daily life it's simply impossible to separate a child's development into tidy, clearly demarcated components. Indeed, parents often have real difficulty in sorting out developmental causes from effects in the lives of their children. For instance, if a girl suddenly starts having troubles at school, is it because of fights she's been having with her best friend, or because of worries brought on by a sibling's illness, or because the assignments in math class have become more difficult, or because she's feeling physically awkward after growing three inches in two months? How are the parents to know where their daughter's problems began, and how to help her overcome them?

Often children themselves do not fully understand or verbally communicate how they feel about the major developmental changes they are experiencing. But their dreams regularly express these feelings, giving parents invaluable insights that can be used to help their children get through the most difficult passages and transitions involved in growing up. Sharing dreams can be a wonderfully effective means of honest emotional communication between parents and children, particularly at those exciting yet frightening times when a child is going through a sudden new spurt of growth and development.

6

DREAMS AND THE
CHANGING FAMILY

DIVORCE, ADOPTION, BLENDED FAMILIES,
AND NEW SIBLINGS

The monster climbed into my house and ate up my baby sister.[1] *—Four-year-old boy with new sister*

I dreamed my mom and dad got married again. —Seven-year-old girl whose parents recently divorced

DREAMING INTENSIFIES FOR BOTH CHILDREN AND adults when family patterns shift. The birth or adoption of a sibling, an elderly grandparent moving into the family home, a teenager leaving for college can all lead to worrisome dreams. The enduring impact of a contested divorce or the difficult adjustment to a changing stepfamily will all be reflected over months and years in the symbolism of a child's dreams. Dreams with themes about feeling left out, being trapped by invaders or kidnappers, searching in strange houses, all embody the normal psychological insecurities that accompany a major alteration in the family constellation.

We all hold within ourselves reassuring images of our family and close friends. When our emotional ties are stable, these images help us maintain a sense of security and safety. However, changes in the patterns of close relationships often provoke anxiety, even when the changes are expected.

Nightmares related to divorce or stepfamily issues may also provoke guilt and anxiety in parents who have done everything they could think of to help their child. Exploring these divorce- or stepfamily-related dreams will help parents understand more clearly how their child is struggling mightily—and perhaps successfully—to cope with massive insecurities.

Take That Baby Back to the Hospital

The birth or adoption of a child produces powerful and often mixed reactions in older siblings. An only child who is emotionally secure may long for or even beg for a baby brother or sister, imagining him or her to be a better companion than the best teddy bear. Of course, they don't factor the sleepless nights and dirty diapers into their fantasy. Nor do they anticipate their parents and relatives cooing and fawning over someone else. Nevertheless, some older siblings have dreams expressing their excitement and wonder about the baby growing in their mommy's tummy and their apparent willingness to welcome the anticipated new arrival. Some children's fantasies and dreams also spin some wild, yet endearing fantasies in a struggle to understand where babies come from.

Five-year-old Brittany had been pleading with her parents for a baby sister ever since she was two. When her mother, Becky, finally became pregnant, Brittany was beside herself with joy. She was especially keen on feeling the baby's movement during the middle phase of the pregnancy. She was very active in playing out scenarios related to nurturing a baby and insisted that her parents buy her a toy stroller. She would spend hours fixing the blankets and outfits for various dolls and her special stuffed rabbit. They would be walked and rocked and fed with toy bottles many times every day.

At the height of her playful rehearsals and simulations of being a mom and a sister, Brittany had a vivid dream and came running into her parents' bedroom practically shouting it.

M O M M Y H A S T W I N S

Mommy, I dreamed you had two babies just like me. I was in the hospital where the doctors keep all the babies and you and Dad came in and saw me and another baby just like me. You asked the doctor if you could keep us both.

Brittany immediately asked, "Mommy, are you going to have twins and will you be able to take care of all of us and still read me stories at night?" Becky explained that there was going to be only one baby, and she would make sure that either she or Dad would always read a story to her every night. Brittany did not seem fully reassured. She continued: "Will you still give me a bath and put me in my pajamas and tuck me in?"

Brittany's dream was the first direct expression of any

ambivalence about the birth of her sibling. All of her prior play activities related to the baby had an overtly positive tone. However, the dream helped Becky and her husband, Todd, realize that Brittany was worried about being displaced and wanted to be the baby who would get all the attention. In addition, despite various carefully worded explanations about where babies come from, Brittany's dream suggested that she still believed that doctors and hospitals issue babies to parents.

At the time of the dream, Becky complimented her daughter on having such a vivid dream about the baby being born, and pointed out that she was the first one in the family to have such a dream. She also reassured Brittany that they would take equally good care of both her and her sister.

Later, when Becky and Todd discussed the dream and watched Brittany play with her doll stroller, they realized that Brittany was both happy to finally have a sister but also worried that she would no longer be the center of attention. Her dream of twins illustrates the unconscious, problem-solving function of dreams. It highlights the anxiety about being displaced by restoring her to the center of her parents' attention. If she was a newborn twin as her dream portrayed, they would surely have to pay equal attention to her!

After discussing the dream, Becky and Todd encouraged Brittany to draw the dream and paid special compliments to her drawing. They used the drawings and playful discussions of the dream image of the twins to gently raise the topic of her worries about being left out when the new baby arrives. They arranged for Brittany to attend a sibling birth preparation class at the local hospital and also planned gatherings with other families that had older and younger siblings.

Despite parental reassurances, one of the most common and troubling responses to the birth of a sibling is rivalry—a fear of being displaced and a sometimes desperate sense of competition. Younger children are especially vulnerable and may regress to earlier behaviors, such as bed-wetting or even asking for a bottle again. Kids of all ages may become extremely sensitive to any form of perceived slight, such as not getting their turn or their adequate share of time with their parents, a special privilege, or a favorite dessert. Upsetting dreams are often one of the first signs that an older child is suffering from sibling rivalry.

In his book *Children's Dreams in Clinical Practice*,[2] Stephen Catalano emphasizes how dreams help facilitate communication between the child and his therapist, especially when a child is unaware or out of touch with his or her feelings. He described how exploring the content of a dream helped an eight-year-old girl adjust to her mother's remarriage and the recent birth of a second half-sibling. Catalano's young patient had been "extremely close and mutually dependent" upon her mother during the unhappy marriage, separation, and remarriage. Now that her mother had a new husband and two babies, she no longer felt important to her mother. Shortly after therapy began, she dreamed:

THE SAD LITTLE DUCK'S
BAD DAY

A little duck lived by himself in a small house below the ground. The duck was sad because he was having a very bad day. He spilled his drink because the glass was so full. Then the ice cream fell off his ice cream

> *cone and later, when he was eating, the picks [tines]*
> *fell out of his fork.*

Although it was hard for her to discuss her feelings directly, she was able to say that she felt just like the duck. And, like the sad little duck in her dream, she felt displaced —relegated to a hovel below the ground. She also felt that absolutely everything was going wrong. Even ice cream, which is normally a treat, was lost and spoiled, and the very fork for eating was disintegrating before her eyes.

As a result of being able to express her feelings about the duck in her dream, she was able to talk to the therapist, and shortly afterward to her parents, about her sadness and sense of abandonment. The resulting breakthrough led to a rapid resolution of her emotional difficulties within six more family therapy sessions.[3]

In a more extreme example of sibling rivalry, Harry, a patient of psychoanalyst John Mack,[4] suffered from both nightmares and aggressive behavior toward his siblings and his parents. He was three and a half years old when his third younger sibling, and only brother, was born. During his mother's last pregnancy, Harry began having serious difficulties controlling his anger. He was repeatedly disciplined for hitting his siblings and stealing their toys. He even punched his mother in the abdomen and threatened to kill the new baby. His parents tried everything, including scoldings, spankings, time-outs, and letting Harry sleep in bed with them.

Shortly after his youngest brother's birth, Harry appeared extremely sad. He began to suck his thumb and regressed in his toilet training, which had been completed a year earlier. He also began to have sleep disturbances and terrifying, violent nightmares, often featuring a girl who had come to hurt him or a woman who had killed him. He was convinced that his dreams were real, and despite his parents' hugs and reassurance, he was inconsolable after the nightmares.

Mack, in trying to help Harry and his parents, used play and fantasy in the therapy sessions to help work out the boy's sense of exclusion. Harry's play was both overtly aggressive and filled with worries about injuries to himself. His dreams, however, portrayed him as the victim of threats and aggression and not as a perpetrator. In children and even in grown-ups, difficult feelings in dreams may be reversed or projected onto characters. Mack viewed Harry's dreams of being a victim of violence as a projection of the boy's rage at being displaced by so many siblings in such a short time.

The above example is clearly an extreme case. Few older siblings will need to see a psychotherapist purely as a result of rivalry toward a new sibling, and most children will have a blend of both positive and negative feelings toward their baby brother or sister. Nevertheless, anyone who has younger siblings may identify with some of Harry's rival-rous feelings.

When parents are caught up in their own positive antic-ipation of the birth of a child, they may miss the onset of worries in their other children. One of the first signs of rivalry comes through dreams.

Dreams of Children of Divorce

Half of all children will experience divorce and many will endure insecurity and stress before, during, and after the break-up. Subsequently, as both of their parents date and remarry, they may acquire new stepsiblings and later half-siblings. In some cases, the new family configuration may be more nurturing and harmonious than the one presided over by their birth parents. In other cases, children are caught in the crossfire of their parents' lingering animosity or are inadvertently neglected as their mothers and fathers undergo overwhelming emotional or financial stress.

Children of divorce are vulnerable to nightmares during the period immediately following the separation and later in response to acute divorce-related conflicts between their parents. Postdivorce dreams clearly reflect the nature of the child's adjustment to the emotional rigors of losing their original family and then changing all of the relationships they had counted on for security.

A widespread theme in these children's conscious thoughts, daydreams, and nocturnal dreams is the wish and hope that their parents might reunite. It is not surprising that this theme is a dominant one in younger children who have recently experienced divorce. However, even teenagers whose parents have remarried or children whose parents are bitterly estranged have persistent dreams of reunions. Exploring these and other divorce-related dreams will help parents understand that their child is struggling and beginning to cope successfully with massive insecurities.

All of the students in a second-grade class were asked to have their parents write down for them one of their dreams on a particular night. Two-thirds of the students returned the next day with dreams. Although the contents of the dreams were fascinating, one theme stood out among the four students whose parents had divorced within the previ-

ous two years: a wished-for reunion of the parents. Two of
these reunion dreams follow:

REUNION

*My dream was about my mom and dad and that the
divorce was all better and they were happy again.*

LONELY AGAIN

*Everyone was sleeping in a big bed with me, my two
older sisters, my mom and my dad. All of a sudden,
I noticed that everyone went back to their own beds to
go to sleep. I stayed under my blankets with my teddy
bear. I was really feeling lonely.*

The first dream clearly fulfills the unconscious and probably conscious wish to undo the trauma of the divorce,
reunite the family, and heal their psyche. The second
dream, "Lonely Again," has more complexity and shows a
graphic image of reunification. It also replays the separation that follows each parental visit. Condensed in the
dream are both memories of the warmth of his parents'
love and an acute replay of the grief and loneliness of missing his mom or dad when he's with the other parent.

Reunion dreams may provoke guilt and anxiety in a
divorced parent who feels they have done everything they
could think of to help their child. Parents should try to set
aside their guilt, listen empathetically to the dreams, and
use them as indicators of feelings related to the divorce.
Talking about the dream may be a safer way to communicate conflicted feelings, including grief, torn loyalty, and
general anxieties.

Soon after a marital separation, children's insecurities

run high. Ten-year-old Brian, whose "Poison Gas" night-mare was explored in chapter four, had always been sensitive to the plight of the disadvantaged. Despite his young age, he worried about homeless people, disaster victims, and the plight of people with AIDS. Brian's precocious social concerns and his general anxieties increased when he learned his father was moving out and divorcing his mother.

Brian may have sensed his parents' increasing estrangement, since he began having worries and upsetting dreams before the actual separation. Then his nightmares increased during the weeks following the separation, as Brian and his brother Jake began spending weekends at his father's new home.

One night, when his mother was tucking him in before sleep, Brian asked if they could buy a rather expensive gift for one of his best friends' birthdays. Gina explained to her son that finances had become tight because of the divorce. Brian immediately became nervous and wanted repeated reassurances from Gina that they would never become like the homeless people he had seen on the street. Even though Gina promised that would never happen, Brian insisted that she couldn't guarantee it. Gina rephrased her offer to "I will do everything in my power to make sure we are never homeless." Brian finally began to calm down and eventually was able to fall asleep. His worries persisted, however, and were expressed that night in the following dream:

LOST AND CRYING

I am wandering around in a really old house with walls that are practically falling down on me. I keep looking everywhere for my mom and my brother and my dad, but no one answers. I start crying and I feel like I am never going to find anyone and finally I wake up and I really am crying.

Gina comforted her son and wiped away his tears and her own. She, too, felt the loneliness and confusion her son's dream so poignantly expressed. Having explored her own dreams for many years, Gina knew that it was important to empathize with the dreamer's feelings. She responded by reflecting back to her son some of her own responses: "If that were my dream, I would feel really lonely and scared." Brian responded with more tears. "Yes, I miss Dad when he's not here and I miss you when I'm at his house. I'd rather just be in my own bed and have both of you here."

Remembering the previous night's discussion about homelessness, Gina knew that Brian would see right through any false promises. "I don't think Daddy and I are going to live together again, but we are going to try hard to stay friends and neither of us would ever leave you alone like you were in the dream."

Brian reiterated how frightened he had been wandering around "that old house" and not finding anyone to help him. Gina suggested that Brian try to imagine that he was back in the dream, so they could work together to think up new endings. Brian eagerly took his mother's invitation to fantasize and began describing an old house that was "all gross like the Addams Family with spider webs everywhere and squeaky floors." As if a lightbulb had gone off, he suddenly exclaimed, "I know. I'll find the phone and call your pager and you can call Nine-one-one, Mom!" Gina had

gotten a pager after the separation, expressly for the purpose of allowing her sons to contact her in an emergency.
This dream solution seemed immensely satisfying to Brian,
who had indeed paged his mother in recent weeks just for
a reassurance call.

This was not Brian's last postdivorce nightmare, as
many months of adjustment lay ahead for the whole family. However, Brian always came to his mother after a
nightmare, eager to have her comfort him and brainstorm
solutions to his dream dilemmas. And although Gina was
upset every time Brian had nightmares, she felt that their
sessions discussing and rehearsing solutions to the dreams
were not only enjoyable for both of them but they helped
her stay alert to Brian's divorce-related anxieties.

Whereas Brian's parents' separation was painful but relatively amicable, ten-year-old Alexander's parents had
been squabbling for many years. He had two recurring
nightmares that began shortly after the divorce, six years
earlier.

Alexander's mother remarried a man with two older
sons, and he and his younger brother got along well with
his new stepbrothers. Alexander's father had not fared so
well following the divorce. He had difficulty maintaining
steady work and seemed to be in a constant rage against
his ex-wife. He made it his mission in life to bad-mouth
Alexander's mother and to fight for increased custody. He
cursed at her, called her a slut and other derogatory names,
and even threatened to take out a gun if Alexander's stepfather came to his house to pick him up.

Although the family court judge had reduced visits with
his father to two overnight visits per month, Alexander
would go through a cycle of tension and irritability for

days before and after his visits to his father. He did not want to end the visits, because he was afraid of both disappointing and angering his father, whom he feared could hurt him or his mother.

Alexander's distress about the visits to his father became so acute that he began misbehaving at school. He refused to turn in assignments, was insolent to teachers, and had angry outbursts at home. He also began to have a horrible, repetitive nightmare.

SUFFOCATION

It's the middle of the night and I feel like I am pushed down on the bed. I can't breathe and I can't wake up and I can't endure it. I wake up right after that.

Suffocation is a universal nightmare theme. For Alexander, the nightmares had become unbearable and his hostility and antisocial behavior in school had resulted in two suspensions and the threat of expulsion from school. When Alexander was brought for psychotherapy, he was not enthusiastic about the idea and did not hide his resistance. He refused to talk about his visits with his father and was protective of any questions that even vaguely suggested any negative appraisal of his father's behavior. His defensiveness is typical of many children of divorce, who feel torn apart by their loyalty to each of their divorced parents and unwilling to reveal any details that would hurt either parent.

When he learned, however, that dreams and nightmares could be part of the therapy, he became intrigued. He talked about his suffocation dreams and wanted to know why he was having them. He also recounted one other repetitive nightmare that he had been having as far back as he could remember. He had had the dream again the night before the therapy session.

TIME BOMB
I can hear this ticktock sound and I can hear the foot-steps. I am looking from the view of the guy with the bomb and hearing what he hears. The sounds are get-ting louder and louder and all of a sudden it explodes.

The dream expresses Alexander's difficulty controlling his anger and his sense of loss of control related to his father's unquenchable rage toward his mother. He was both afraid of his father's anger and worried that he, too, might be unable to control his own anger.

The fact that the dream had occurred immediately after the visit to his father was of great interest to the therapist. This led to a discussion with Alexander about the distress he felt before, during, and after his visits with his father. This was a topic that he had refused to discuss prior to sharing the dream in therapy.

Exploring the dream helped Alexander feel more com-fortable to begin discussing his mixed feelings—the fact that he was frightened of his father's violent threats, swear-ing, and tendency to neglect him during their visits.

The following week, Alexander requested that his mother sit in on his therapy session, and he revealed more of his fears to her and asked if it was possible to visit his father less often. Alexander told her that he was scared of his father's temper and had bad dreams right after the vis-its. He asked for shorter visits without sleeping over.

Over the next month, through a continuing series of discussions with Alexander and separately with his mother and stepfather, a plan was made to reduce visitation to two short visits per month. Within three months Alexander's behavior problems at school had decreased dramatically. He was still occasionally defiant, but he was no longer facing suspensions and referrals to the principal. He no longer had dreams of bombs or suffocation, but occasionally he did have nightmares of being trapped by a criminal.

Dreams reveal the valiant inner struggles that a child is making to adjust and form new images of family that will give him or her security and fulfillment. Exploring dreams during these stressful periods will help diagnose the child's difficulties and can become part of the solution as you begin to talk about the forbidden or difficult topics that dreams inevitably bring to awareness.

Adopted Children Dream of Their Birth Parents

When Jana, an adopted girl of ten, began having recurring dreams about her birth parents, her adoptive parents, Hal and Jessica, were dismayed and perplexed. They had always tried to be open about the fact that she was adopted, but the dreams were so persistent that they began to interpret them as a rejection of their love and loyalty to their daughter. They feared that Jana would insist upon meeting her birth mother, whom they felt would be a disruptive influence.

When Hal and Jessica learned that such dreams did not imply rejection, they were relieved and became more open and curious. Such dreams and parental reactions are actually *normal* for adopted children and represent their intermittent struggle to come to terms with their identity and sense of being different. Adopted children may at times be preoccupied with feelings of rejection by their birth parents and fears of rejection by their adoptive parents. Knowing this, Hal and Jessica became more open and curious about Jana's dreams related to her birth parents.

One of Jana's most distressing dreams involved being kidnapped by her birth father, about whom Hal and Jessica had no information:

> ### MY REAL DAD TRIES TO KIDNAP ME
> *I was in a court with an old, mean-looking judge. Everyone is getting loud, like they are all going to start fighting. The judge is really, really mad and is shouting for everyone to be quiet. This big guy in the back tries to grab me and is pulling me out of the courtroom, yelling, "Jana is mine. I'm her real dad and I'm taking her home." I could see outside and he had a car out there waiting with a lady and some other kids inside. I kept trying to get away but he was squeezing my arm so hard and he kept dragging me. I screamed at the judge hoping he would see me but no one seemed to notice.*

Jana's parents learned that she had recently watched a television newsmagazine focusing on controversies surrounding cases of adopted children who are returned to their birth parents due to legal technicalities such as a father who wasn't properly notified of paternity prior to the adoption. In addition, along with normal fears of the dark, Jana had at times suffered from anxieties about getting lost or separated from her parents and being kidnapped.

Although she had never mentioned the television show,

it had been bothering her for weeks as she worried that her birth father might return and take her away from her adoptive parents. Hal and Jessica reassured Jana with both the legal facts—her adoption was finalized within months after her birth—and the emotional facts—they cherished her and would never reject her or give her up. Jana began sobbing and was genuinely relieved. She also went on to tell Hal and Jessica about many other ideas, impressions, and misconceptions about adoption that she had picked up from television, overhearing adult conversations, and from other adopted children.

By sympathetically listening to the details of Jana's dream, Hal and Jessica realized that due to their own fears, they were poorly handling discussions about adoption with Jana. Their own sensitivity about being rejected by Jana had blinded them to the underlying themes in her dream—her anxieties about separation and rejection due in part to her adopted status.

Hal and Jessica were impressed at how transparently Jana's dream expressed important issues and feelings that she had been unable to communicate verbally. They were not only able to reassure her, but discussing the dream made them contemplate a series of other stressful events that may have accentuated Jana's fears and set off her nightmares.

Besides the distress of watching the television show on adoption controversies, the parents of Jana's best friend had recently separated. Then, during the summer, the family had visited Hal's parents after his father had a mild heart attack. These issues, they came to realize, were probably troubling to Jana and were ripe for further discussion and clarification.

Hal and Jessica bought some books on adoption for children, sought out a support group for adoptive parents, and went for a short series of sessions with a family therapist just to assure themselves that Jana's concerns about separation and adoption were not part of a more severe psychological syndrome.

Inspired by the illuminating discussions that flowed from Jana's nightmare, Hal and Jessica also took much more interest in her dreams and their own. Although her dreams about her birth parents did not recur in the year following her nightmares, they did occasionally have themes of separation anxiety from her adoptive mother or exclusion by friends. She completed a series of watercolor paintings about her separation dreams, one of which Jana and Hal framed and hung in her bedroom.

As with divorce-related dreams, adopted children's dreams may at times alert parents to the need for further discussion and clarification of inner conflicts related to adoption, identity, birth parents, and even more fundamental fears about separation and abandonment.

When any major change occurs in the family, children's dreams serve as a sensitive gauge of unresolved feelings and conflicts. An important advantage of dreams is that they hint at exactly when the child is ready to discuss an issue and give clues to what aspect of an issue is bothering the child. As families evolve and change, children's dreams illustrate to parents the valiant efforts their children are making to comprehend what is happening and form new family images that will give them renewed security and fulfillment.

FIRST AID FOR CRISIS
DREAMS

DREAM PATTERNS IN RESPONSE TO CRISIS,
INJURY, DISABILITY, ABUSE, AND GRIEF

I had a dream that I was in the middle of the water all alone, drowning, I was calling and yelling for help but nobody heard me.—A four-year-old who had been repeated sexually abused by his adolescent brother[1]

D REAMS ARE A CRUCIAL PART OF THE HUMAN REAC-tion to family crises, natural disasters, illnesses, injuries, and other traumas. In the aftermath of a trauma, vivid and repetitive dreams can and should be expected. Posttraumatic dreams focus relentlessly on the crisis a child is facing. With some distortions and transformations, they are often like flashbacks of the troubling event—replaying and usually exaggerating the overwhelming emotions connected to the trauma.

Regrettably, these posttraumatic nightmares seem to add insult to emotional injury. They are acutely distressing; their content may seem perplexing; and it is hard for parents to see their value. As a result, along with their children, parents are tempted to ignore, avoid, or forget these horrific reminders of a difficult event or situation.

Crisis nightmares, however, present an extraordinary opportunity. Sharing and exploring event-related dreams with their parents or helping professionals gives children a chance to express raw, painful feelings and needs, and to receive the understanding and comfort they so desperately yearn for in times of dire emotional crisis. Especially for younger children, who don't yet have the words to discuss their reactions to a traumatic experience, exploring dreams during a period of family crisis is an ideal way to express their need for extra attention and reassurance. By playfully exploring the symbols and metaphors of a disturbing dream, a child's resulting drawings, dramatizations, and verbal elaborations can provide a pathway to healing the raw wounds of grief and trauma.

When children's crisis nightmares, and the stresses connected with them, do not receive adequate attention and empathy, the emotional conflicts may go underground. The lingering nightmares that follow can become a crucial signal that the child and the family have reached an impasse in recovering from a traumatic event.

The value of crisis nightmares, even when they persist, is that they provide parents with a series of opportunities to understand which conflicts related to a recent trauma are still bothering the child and how far the child has progressed in his or her emotional recovery. Posttraumatic dreams can help parents understand the stage of emotional recovery their child has reached in working out a trauma. Repetitive and unchanging dreams may signal an unresolved trauma. However, evidence in the dreams of fighting back (e.g., struggling actively against threatening animals) can be a healthy sign that the child is beginning to cope with the shattering impact of a trauma. Such dreams not only *reflect* but may actually *enhance* the psyche's gradual, evolving efforts to heal.

As you learn more about patterns in crisis dreams in this chapter and begin to understand and explore your children's dreams during stressful times, keep in mind the following crucial guidelines:

- Dreams are more vivid during life's crises and turning points.
- Nightmares are more frequent, persistent, and distressing after a trauma.
- No matter how illogical, distorted, or gruesome, post-traumatic dreams form part of the human struggle to recover from events that threaten our sense of emotional and physical survival.
- Crisis dreams give parents an opportunity to understand and help their child navigate the stages of emotional recovery from a traumatic event.
- With reassurance, empathy, and playful exploration, posttraumatic nightmares are not only curable but can become a springboard for healing the emotional blocks that crises create.

Patterns in Children's Posttraumatic Dreams

Lenore Terr's fascinating book on childhood trauma, *Too Scared to Cry,*[2] documents the childhood dreams of a number of trauma survivors and includes her extensive work with the survivors of the Chowchilla, California, kidnap-ping, wherein a group of children were kidnapped and buried alive inside their school bus. Although all of the children survived, many suffered repetitive nightmares for years afterward. In her book, Terr describes four repetitive patterns of posttraumatic dreams: exact repetitions; modi-fied repetitions; deeply disguised dreams; and terror dreams that cannot be remembered upon wakening.

Exact repetitions are a bit of a misnomer; other studies (and Terr herself) have shown that trauma survivors rarely or never have dreams that repeat the *exact* memory of a trauma. As an example of what Terr calls an exact repeti-tion dream, she cites the dreams of an English girl named Tina, the niece of the pianist Ralph Vaughan Williams. During the Nazi bombings of London, she and her family moved to her uncle's country home to avoid the bombings. At about the age of four, she began to develop repetitive nightmares and conscious fantasies about being out in a garden and "a burning plane was falling on top of her." Young Tina asked her mother if the event had ever occurred, but either her mother denied it or she didn't ask in the right way. Finally, when she was about ten and still suffering the nightmare, she was told that a plane had fallen in a field near her uncle's house. Following this clari-fication, the dreams decreased in frequency and stopped within a year.[3]

While Terr labeled these dreams an exact repetition, in reality the dreams twisted the memory of the event slightly by representing the plane as crashing on the house on top of her. In Alan's study of the posttraumatic dreams of the 1991 Oakland firestorm survivors, few if any dreams por-trayed accurate renditions of the experience, most dreams distorting some or all aspects of the fire and its aftermath. The fire, which in reality was a fast-moving wall of flames as high as one hundred feet, was represented in some survivors' dreams as a ferocious animal and in others as a devastating flood of water, and not as a wall of fire. The images are parallel in that both the fire and the water symbolism depict monumental, natural forces that are impersonal and destructive.[4]

Posttraumatic dreams that are modified repetitions are probably easier to identify as related to a trauma when compared with deeply disguised dreams. The Chowchilla kidnap survivors studied by Terr had many modified repetitions, such as a seven-year-old girl who dreamed about the terror of the burial phase of the kidnapping through a dream that she "was in an alligator hole and the alligator bit" her.

Deeply disguised dreams are harder to connect with a crisis or traumatic event. Freud promoted the notion that the content or surface level of a dream is more likely to be a disguise of the dream's true meanings. Contemporary psychologists and dream researchers no longer consider every dream a camouflage of its true meanings. Dreams fall on a continuum, with some aspects of a dream's meaning disguised and distorted while others are directly expressed in the imagery. For example, a firestorm survivor who lost her home dreamed about being burned by a plumbing pipe. Later she dreamed of attempting to douse a campfire. These modified distortions of the real trauma did not occur; they are symbols of the dreamer's struggle to overcome lingering fears connected to the fire. Deeply disguised posttraumatic dreams may well serve to protect us from the disturbing memory of the real event until we have recovered enough to face what we fear directly.

Terror dreams that cannot be remembered may be some of the most horrifying, especially for younger children who wake up feeling amorphous, suffocating fear. Although they may not have the other characteristics of a night terror (occurring early in the night accompanied by screaming, shaking, and an inability to be roused), they are similar to night terrors in that they don't have a story attached. These contentless, blank nightmares must be taken seriously as a warning sign of a level of distress felt at the deepest level of body and soul. When the dreamer of blank nightmares is nourished with attention and empathy, he or she may begin to feel secure enough to tolerate remembering a story to go with the terror in subsequent dreams.

Posttraumatic dreams are shaped by the nature and severity of the crisis a child has endured. No matter how disguised or confusing the nightmare, try to connect the symbols and story to the events your child has experienced. The ideas and insights you generate will give you inspiration to help your frightened child assert his or her needs and overcome the aftermath of the crisis.

Natural Disasters

When a natural disaster such as an earthquake, tornado, fire, or flood strikes, those children who are the most directly exposed to the disaster are more likely to have the most severe nightmares and sleep disturbances as well as behavioral symptoms. Children who are farther away and less directly threatened may have nightmares, but they are generally less destructive or life threatening.

Tornadoes, with deadly swirling winds in excess of two hundred miles an hour, can toss cars like toys, crumble buildings within seconds, and snuff the life from people and animals in their path. Psychologist Kathleen Nader reported on the psychological aftermath of a tornado that destroyed part of a school and killed nine children.[5] She observed that nightmares, which could be called "deeply disguised" (using Terr's classification scheme), served to protect the children from having to face overwhelming aspects of the trauma.

One third-grader had monster dreams after suffering a fractured foot in the tornado. Upon seeing a wall falling, the girl had tried to run for safety. A friend grabbed her foot, ostensibly to help her hide under a table, and she tripped and her leg was crushed. She was angry at her friend but afraid to express it because the friend had been severely injured and she was afraid of losing her friendship. As a result, she became upset with her mother and began having monster nightmares. The monsters may have been exaggerated representations of the anger she wouldn't allow herself to express at her friend. When she finally talked to a therapist about her anger, her monster dreams stopped.

Nightmares may become an issue, even for people who are not direct victims of a disaster. The fortunate survivors of an auto accident, crime scene, or natural disaster may suffer guilt about having survived while others perished. These lucky survivors are usually afflicted with anxieties and bad dreams depicting exaggerated versions of what might have happened to them.

After the Oakland firestorm of 1991, children whose homes were spared heard graphic details about the deadly fire and the injuries and destruction it caused. They were also repeatedly exposed to images of the fire and the destruction it caused through the extensive television coverage. Even though these children were not burned and did not experience material losses, they and their parents experienced a flurry of nightmares similar to, and in some cases worse than, those of the actual victims of that urban wildfire. Lucky survivors appear to be a lot more at risk for nightmares and other posttraumatic symptoms than was previously thought.

Parents may suffer from depression or posttraumatic stress disorder themselves. When they are too overwhelmed to be alert to the disaster's impact on their children, nightmares and other symptoms may result. Melissa's mom nearly became immobilized at the moment the firefighters were insisting on a total evacuation of her neighborhood. It was twelve-year-old Melissa, screaming at her mother during the fire, insisting that they throw the last few belongings in the trunk and head for safety, who saved the family.

Melissa and her family lost their home and nearly all their belongings in the fire. Although their loss was covered by insurance, they had to stay with friends for a few weeks and then in a smaller rented home for over two years while their house was being rebuilt. Melissa's mother was depressed after the fire and suffered from a severe form of emotional numbing that is common in trauma survivors. Melissa herself, within a few weeks of the fire, began having a recurring fire nightmare that continued off and on for almost a year.

BURNING TREES

The fire is coming again and I can hear little explosions in the treetops. I can see the flames and smell the smoke and I am afraid the fire is going to drop down and set my hair and clothes on fire. I yell to my mom: "Let's get out of here!" She acts like she doesn't hear me at all, so I start screaming, "Mom! Mom!" and wake just before the flames hit me.

Melissa's dreams replicated some real memories of the sight and sound and smell of burning trees as the fire quickly spread through the hills around her house. Many other survivors were also troubled by waking flashbacks of pinecones overhead crackling and exploding as the firestorm ignited the tall trees in the hills.

The worst part of the dream for Melissa was not the fire but her mother's emotional paralysis. The horror of the fire was dreadful but not as frightening as the loss of trust in her mother's protective instincts. Even after the fire, Melissa's mother was preoccupied with her own depression and not fully responsive to Melissa's nagging anxieties and dream disturbances.

Hearing about the support groups and therapy sessions some of her friends were attending, Melissa requested that her parents take her to a therapist so she could talk about her nightmares and other worries. In her first session of therapy, she talked about her burning tree nightmares and her sense of disappointment and anger at her mother. While she may have soon focused on those topics, her nightmares provided a point of entry for the therapist to understand the core issues from the fire that were plaguing Melissa.

Recovery from Grief

Dreams are one of the first steps in the process of mourning following the death of a loved one. When a child's grandparent or other relative dies or even after the death of an important pet, dreams and nightmares can give parents crucial information about how their child is responding and coping with the loss.

In some Asian-Pacific tribes, dreaming is considered inextricable from the grieving process. For the Negrito tribe of the Philippines, the spirit of a dead person is expected to return to visit his or her offspring and the funeral feast is always delayed until the spirit of the dead person, in the form of a ghost, has made several visits and negotiated with the offspring about the size and timing of the feast.[6]

Most religions offer rituals to give solace, meaning, and structure during a period of mourning a loss. These rituals offer many psychological benefits to the bereaved. They bring together the family to provide mutual emotional support. They instill meaning and uplift the bereaved just when they feel demoralized and shattered. And they acknowledge the slow pace of human grief by staging the observances gradually over a period of time to prevent the grief process from being hidden from view.

A flurry of vivid, disturbing, and sometimes repetitive dreams are common after a loss. Soon after a death, dreams of threatening ghosts and vampires, morbid scenes of corpses and coffins, and painful rejections and separations may exacerbate or even predominate over a child's conscious feelings of loss. Or conversely, the dreams may have an intense spiritual significance (see chapter eight) for the dreamer.

After a death, the inability of children under eight to fully differentiate dreaming from reality is compounded by their inability to fully understand the irreversibility of death. Therefore, when children encounter a recently deceased relative in a dream, they may experience confusion and anguish both within the dream and upon waking.

Despite their troubling nature, these haunting grief dreams offer parents crucial clues about their child's response to the loss. Exploring these dreams can provide parents with a valuable vehicle for easing the grief process and helping children navigate the stages of recovering from the loss of a relative, friend, or pet.

An especially devastating loss for a family is when a baby dies from sudden infant death syndrome (SIDS). With no advance warning, an apparently healthy infant dies. The older child is no longer a big brother or sister; his or her parents are in shock; and the family may be reeling from the loss for months or years to come. Divorce rates have been found to be extraordinarily high in the years following the death of a child.

In the eerie aftermath, night terrors, nightmares, and fears of the dark are common as children, who may not fully comprehend the meaning of death, try to cope with loss and a radical change in the family structure. The dream of a three-year-old suggested that she (like many parents) may be blaming herself for the death.

A Monster Is Coming

A monster is coming to take her because she had killed her baby brother.[7]

Another young child had a dream of a monster taking her up to heaven to be with her brother. This dream suggests confusion about the boundaries between life and death as well as grief and a wish to join her departed brother. Similar dreams of joining relatives in heaven or other forms of spiritual reunions are also common in the grief dreams of adults.

After his favorite uncle, Matthew, was killed in a motorcycle accident, five-year-old Ian began having frequent nightmares and night terrors. He also became moody, crying more easily and occasionally wetting his bed. His uncle Matt, the youngest of his father's brothers, was a student at the local university and used to take Ian out once or twice a month for movies, ice cream, and other activities. He had even ridden on his uncle's motorcycle a couple of times and had bragged to his friends about his uncle's Harley.

At first, Ian refused to give any details about his dreams, asserting that they were "too scary" and he wished they would go away. Gradually, as his disturbed sleep continued, he was encouraged to talk about his nightmares as a way to help make them go away or at least not worry him as much. With that gentle persuasion, he reluctantly confided a dream that was bothering him.

HOLDING ON TO UNCLE MATT
I'm riding on the back of Uncle Matt's Harley and we're going faster and faster and I am holding on as tight as I can. All of a sudden, we start to fly off a big bridge. I'm falling way, way, way down to the water. I scream, "Matt, Matt, help me!" I'm choking in the

*water. I can't find him anywhere! I'm screaming
"Help! Help!" but nobody comes to get me out.*

Ian's first tearful question after he finished telling the
dream was, "Is Uncle Matt really dead? I felt like I was
holding on to him like we used to." Ian's parents, also sobbing in response to his dream, reaffirmed that Matt was,
indeed, dead. They reminded him of the funeral that the
whole family had attended a month earlier. "But it seemed
like he was *really* there in my dream." "I know, Ian, I can't
believe it either," Ian's father, Roger, said.

Denial is an inevitable phase in responding to the death
of someone close. The mind plays tricks on us. We think
we hear the dead person's voice or see someone in a crowd
on the street, and when we experience a vivid image of the
deceased in a dream, it can be excruciating to wake up and
face the cruel reality of their absence.

For Ian, dream and reality are muddled. Not only was he
confused about whether his uncle was really gone, but his
dream suggests that he may have unconsciously merged his
own experience of loss with his fantasy of his uncle's experience of death. He had always admired and identified
strongly with his uncle, and in the dream he was facing a
similar mortal danger with his uncle—unconsciously preoccupied with the fear "Am I about to die like my uncle?"
Perhaps the dream, if not shared, may have caused him to
harbor the irrational belief, common in children and
adults, that he may have caused the accidental death by
hanging on too tightly during the dream while they were
falling.

Ian's dream portrayed him desperately but vainly
searching for help while drowning. Dreams often use the

image of drowning to symbolize overwhelming emotions. And Ian, like his parents, was indeed feeling helpless and confused, unable to express his needs to anyone or to be rescued from his overwhelming grief.

Although Ian's parents, Roger and Elaine, had encouraged him to share the details of his dream, it was emotionally wrenching to hear, and reminded them how they had neglected to check in with him during the weeks after Matt's death. Partly due to Ian's dream, Roger and Elaine decided to seek grief counseling to deal with the loss and to be more psychologically available to help Ian deal with his sleep problems and his grief. Within a few weeks, Ian's sleep problems diminished, and although he did occasionally have further nightmares about his uncle, he was more willing to share them with his parents.

Grief dreams progress in stages that emphasize the painful loss at first and gradually show acceptance and the re-creation of treasured moments with the deceased loved one. Almost a year after Matt's death, Ian's nightmares had become very infrequent, and he began having occasional dreams of riding bicycles together with his dad and his uncle. These dreams signaled a resolution of the acute phase of grief, focusing on more pleasant memories of his uncle and his connection to Ian's father. The bicycle dreams had unconsciously solved the "problem" of deadly motorcycle accidents posed by the earlier nightmares, replacing the motorcycles with the more benign vehicles associated with family outings and relationships with important male figures.

Psychotherapist Stephen Catalano described a dream of a seven-year-old boy who was being seen for psychotherapy subsequent to witnessing his younger brother being run over by a car in front of the family home. In the third session, he asked the boy, "Have you had any dreams since our last visit?"[8]

THE BEAR WITH A HUMAN FACE

I was in a big, dark forest and saw something that looked like a bear with a human face. I just stared at it and every time it moved, giant scorpions came out of its face.

In response to the therapist's questions, the boy indicated that the dream was "scary" and that he was alone in the dream and near a fort that he and his mother and some friends had built.

Although the dreamer was not able to discuss the dream any further or expound on his scary feelings, Catalano emphasized that dreams can be used as a basis for understanding a child's grief reactions even when the child is not ready or able to verbally explore the loss. He speculated that the fear connected to the backyard fort might relate to the boy's sense that his house had become a dangerous place where tragedy could strike at any minute. The grotesque face of the bear may have been a distorted symbol of having witnessed the look on his brother's face at the time of death. Many survivors bear vivid memories of isolated visual details from the moment the trauma occurred. These details, such as the look on a person's face, often appear in dreams in a slightly distorted form.

In situations where young children are unable to verbally express overwhelming feelings (in this case guilt, horror, loss, and generalized fear possibly symbolized by the dark forest in the above dream), a parent or grief counselor may use his or her own imagination to elaborate on the child's grief dreams, such as playing with the symbols and trying to make connections to events and feelings associated with the loss. However, parents and therapists should express their explanations in a simple, even tentative, form with no expectation that the child will agree. The goal is not to issue a brilliant interpretation but to convey reassurance and help the child identify and express difficult feelings through the safety of dream symbols.

Most studies of trauma indicate that the more direct a child's exposure to a trauma, the more devastating the impact as evidenced by more persistent and unresolved nightmares. A child that hears about the death of a grandparent they barely knew may be affected, but less so than a child, such as Ian, who had a close relationship with his uncle. The most shattering impact occurs when a child is directly exposed to a trauma, such as witnessing a murder, bombing, or accident that causes fatal injuries to a close family member.[9]

Martín, an eight-year-old Mexican-American boy from Oakland, California, was a psychological victim of the urban plague of crack cocaine. Returning from school one afternoon, he found his sixteen-year-old sister, Leticia, lying dead from an overdose. Although he tried to be brave, helping his hysterical mother during the funeral, the impact could not be hidden.

Martín was identified by his teacher as needing psychological help because he was crying uncontrollably in class; his grades were dropping; and he was losing weight. At first, he wouldn't talk about his sister's death, but instead complained of horrible recurring nightmares. He told his teacher that these terrifying dreams involved seeing his sister at school or on the street and watching her disappear or leave.

THE HAUNTING STARE

I can see my sister, Leticia, at my school. I'm inside but she's still out on the playground staring at me. Her face looks real worried and it scares me.

Martín was referred to a school-based, group psychotherapy program, run by the local community health center. In this group, he conveyed his obsession that his sister wasn't dead but was still haunting the family home. Gradually, he elaborated details of his nightmares. As he talked about them he reported that they became less terrifying and a new theme began to occur in his dreams. In the first of these dreams, his whole family owned a restaurant named after his sister.

LETTY'S PLACE

Our whole family owns a Mexican Restaurant. There is a big sign and I think it's called Leticia's or Letty's Place. My mom and my grandma and my aunties are there. Letty is cooking the frijoles on a huge stove and my whole family is helping her make the burritos and special tamales like we have at Christmas.

The therapist encouraged him to draw his dream and he eagerly agreed, producing a series of drawings that he shared within the group and with his teachers. At his school's open house, the pictures were the first thing he wanted his mother to see.

Martín's mother, who had been pregnant at the time of Leticia's death, gave birth to a girl six months later. Late in the pregnancy, Martín's pictures began to include his baby sister, Maritza. As he continued to talk about his drawings and photos, his depression and his problems concentrating improved, but he was still tempted by the idea that his sister was alive.

Shortly after the birth of his sister, Martín had a breakthrough dream.

Sister's Reunion

It was at our house and when I came home from school, my baby sister crawled out onto the front porch like she was waiting for me. So I picked her up and brought her inside. Everyone was there eating tons of food. And Letty was there smiling and I went right up to her and showed her Maritza and put the baby right up into her arms. She was real, real happy.

Martín talked about this dream in his therapy group and drew a picture that he showed to his therapist, his teacher, and his mother. He felt that his sister Leticia looked peaceful in the dream. He no longer insisted that she was a haunting presence in the house and felt she was a lot happier. He now appeared to begin to accept the reality of her death. His depression lifted dramatically in the weeks following the dream, reflected in the series of drawings of his house and family that were inspired by the dream.

For Martín, his dreams gave him the symbolic vocabulary to express his grief. All of the dreams are infused with his attempt to deny the loss of his sister and the grotesque experience of finding her dead. His initial, repetitive dreams of Leticia staring at him are a classic example of the intrusive imagery that trauma survivors have in dream, fantasy, and waking thought.

As an eight-year-old in posttraumatic shock, he had regressed back to a developmental level where he couldn't distinguish dream from reality. As with bereaved adults, Martín's grief dreams followed an evolution from more unresolved, haunting images to more integrative, healing symbolism as his recovery progressed.

Although his dreams and drawings of the restaurant and home scenes continued to resurrect his sister and give her a central place in the family, the impact of the dreams is more uplifting. And in the culminating dream of this series, Martín has merged the image of his dead sister with his newborn sister. This reunion of the two sisters signals a deeper resolution of his grief and was the final dream in the series.

From this extended vignette, we see the value of tracking a series of dreams for a bereaved or traumatized child. Through the dream sharing, an understanding adult can help a child reassemble shattered pieces of their psyche in a process that follows the inner rhythm of the child's tolerance.

Children who suffer overwhelming experiences of grief, trauma, or severe illness have extremely vivid dreams. Sharing such dreams gives the child a chance to be better understood by his or her caregivers and to express crucial feelings and needs that may bring them recognition and fulfillment during a time of dire emotional crisis.

Illness and Impending Death

Following an accident, an acute bout of a chronic ailment, and even in the throes of a fatal illness, dreams offer parents, health-care providers, and mental health specialists clues about the psychological impact on a child's physical condition. Even when children are too sick or overwhelmed to explore or discuss the specifics of their dreams, the imagery and feelings of the dreams may communicate to an empathic adult what the children cannot express in words.

A ten-year-old girl who had suffered a grand mal epileptic seizure continued to have recurring nightmares for over a year afterward. Her dreams were very simple, almost impersonal images of explosions, sometimes seen from afar and sometimes blowing up all around her. Even though her condition was stable and her seizures controlled by medication, her nightmares indicated how emotionally shattering the experience had been and how vulnerable she still felt to another devastating seizure. An astute neurologist, who was examining her as a follow-up to her seizure, recommended that she also be evaluated to monitor her psychological condition. As a result, her parents, who had focused only on the medical aspects of her epilepsy, began to take a greater interest in the psychological impact. They sought out brief psychotherapy and ended up joining a support group for parents and children with epilepsy.

Roberta, a teenager, suffered from Tourette's syndrome, which is accompanied by facial or body movements, or "tics," and uncontrolled verbalizations that are sometimes profane. Roberta had long-standing difficulties paying attention, following instructions, and controlling her anger and her behavior in general. Although her parents had gone to every specialist and read every book on Tourette's, her mother, Lucy, had been getting more and more frustrated trying to manage the situation. Lucy would occasionally fly off the handle, degrading Roberta's misbehavior.

Roberta was having increasing problems with insomnia and bad dreams. At first, she didn't want to discuss her nightmares, but as they got worse, she finally relented and described her repetitive dream to her uncle Gordon, who had kept a dream journal for many years and had encouraged her to talk about the dreams.

BLACK DOG CHASING ME
A big hairy, black dog is chasing me, barking really loud and trying to kill me. I try to run but I trip and can't get up and the dog starts to bite me from behind.

Gordon could see a look of terror on his niece's face as she told the dream. Having attended and led many dream workshops, he decided that a rescripting approach might alleviate some of Roberta's fears. He encouraged her to imagine a new ending for the dream. With some discussion and encouragement from Gordon, Roberta decided that she would turn and face the attacking dog and give it a hug. Gordon encouraged her to rehearse the new ending in her mind before she went to sleep that night.

The next morning, Roberta reported that she had a dream about the same dog. When she turned around, the dog transformed into her mother. She then hugged her and felt greatly relieved. That dream never returned and her nightmares diminished substantially.

Roberta's dream is a good example of how dreams can

have meanings on more than one level. In part, the dark, hairy dog may have represented her own aggression, which she could not control and which seemed to sneak up on her, attacking her and others with anger and antisocial behavior. The fact that the dog turned out to be her mother in the follow-up dream also suggests that, to Roberta, the angry dog may have symbolized the criticism she felt her mother had been directing at her. Wild animals attacking are very common in younger children's dreams and may symbolize specific fears or a general struggle to learn to control the child's own aggression or attempts to overcome the impact of harsh treatment by adults.

Concerned about his niece's self-esteem and about a vicious cycle developing, Gordon shared Roberta's dream with Lucy. He then explored his ideas about the dream with both Lucy and Roberta. This discussion helped to reduce the tensions between them and led to more positive methods of solving problems between mother and daughter.

When children have battled a grave or debilitating disease, their struggle with survival is reflected in dreams. Ricky Ray, a fifteen-year-old hemophiliac, was mortally ill with AIDS, contracted from a tainted blood transfusion. Due to his disease, he was expelled from school. Then his family's house was burned down in an attempt to force them from the community. The media had documented the family's travails, and he had even received an encouraging call from then President-elect Clinton, who had heard about his plight.

Just weeks before his death he began having a recurring dream:

It's Not My Time, Yet

I dreamed I tried to go through the light. I thought I was going to die, but someone blocked me and pushed me out of the way and said it wasn't my time yet.

This dream, which he described during an interview on CNN,[10] brought sympathy from millions and helped him find hope and solace in his last few weeks of life. It also has key elements that have been recorded in the dreams of adults facing death. There is an acute awareness of time and an accurate sense of the rhythm of the approach of death. Near-death dreams often contain mystical and spiritual symbols, such as the presence of light, symbolizing death and the hereafter.[11]

The language of a dying child's dreams, if listened to by a compassionate adult, can help the child express the overwhelming experience of approaching death. The parent or helping professional can also gain new insights into the child's emotional needs.

Dream Patterns of Abuse Survivors

Child abuse is one of the most devastating blows to a child's basic sense of security. Physical, sexual, and emotional abuse can have an immeasurable and lifelong impact on a child's psychological health, especially when it is perpetrated by a parent, family member, or trusted adult.

Abused children are especially susceptible to violent nightmares of being chased, threatened, injured, or even killed. Being lost, abandoned, or unable to obtain help are other themes linked to abuse. When the dreams of abuse survivors are explored, the characters and setting of their repetitive dreams are often embedded with references, both overt and camouflaged, to the visual characteristics of the abuser and the place where the violation occurred.

The dreams of abuse survivors have age-related variations, such as a child's dreams of a vicious wolf turning into a teen's dream of a dark, threatening figure or an adult's dream of a crazed rapist. This may not be surprising, but what is surprising is that these abuse-related nightmare themes may endure for a lifetime with later variations influenced by the impact of subsequent events and trauma.

The recall of a dream cannot be taken as evidence that abuse has occurred. Nevertheless, where abuse has already been confirmed, dreams, relationship patterns, and behavioral symptoms are dramatically shaped by the trauma.

A study of women during menopause concluded that those who had suffered physical or sexual abuse during childhood continue to have far more dream themes of being persecuted and attacked up to forty years later compared to women who had not suffered abuse.[12]

One of the most fascinating but disturbing studies of abused children's nightmares was conducted in the late 1980s by Harvard Medical School instructor John Weil. He made an in-depth analysis of a hundred clinical case histories and discovered startling patterns by correlating the children's symptoms and dreams with the type of abuse they suffered.[13]

He found that more than two thirds of the children who had experienced sexual abuse had dreams or symptoms pertaining to the eyes. Their dreams involved going blind, looking at and staring at movies, performances, and images involving light bulbs and beams.

Regarding visual dream symbolism and symptoms, Weil

concluded that the horrible sight of what they experienced had caused ongoing sensitivity to what else they might see. Weil also found that when compared with a control group, sexually and physically abused children had significantly more dreams and symptoms related to fire, falling, killing, biting, and cutting.

Lenore Terr writes about novelist Virginia Woolf, who had a childhood nightmare that haunted her from the first time she had it until her death. Although it occurred the day after her mother died, in many ways the dream suggests she was haunted, even fixated, on the repeated sexual abuse she had suffered earlier at the hands of her older half-brothers, Gerald and George Duckworth. Decades later, in her fifties, still struggling with the abuse from her childhood, she wrote about the dream.[14]

THE HORRIBLE FACE OF AN ANIMAL
I was looking in a glass when a horrible face—the face of an animal—suddenly showed over my shoulder.

Terr suggests that the looking glass probably represented what Virginia Woolf had witnessed, and it remained fixed in her mental mirror—the hideous animal instincts in the eyes of her abuser and brother. She was never able to completely shake the insidious reflection of the beast in her dreams or the shattering impact of repeated sadistic abuse in her conscious memories. Although Virginia Woolf was obviously productive as a writer, she struggled with emotional numbing, as well as other symptoms related to the abuse throughout her life. At fifty-nine, two years after writing about the above dream, she drowned herself by weighting herself down with rocks and wading into a river.

Nightmares are certainly not the only lingering symptom for abuse survivors. Included among the many symptoms are anxiety, depression, detachment from feelings, difficulties with close relationships, and self-defeating and even self-destructive behaviors. Abused children, especially those who are victimized by family members or trusted friends, require careful evaluation and treatment to reduce the devastating impact of the trauma.

Nightmares insistently emphasize inner conflicts and traumas that have not yet been resolved. Listening to and gently, creatively exploring nightmares of trauma survivors can lift some of their oppressive grip on the dreamer. Encouraging dream sharing for victims of violence and survivors of other acute crises can help parents and professionals comprehend the emotional burden that lingers for years and decades after the actual abuse. For many, this will lead to more opportunities for transforming the pain through treatment and sympathetic responses from within the family network.

VISIONS OF TRANSCENDENCE

Dreams and the Spiritual Life of Children

————

S PIRITUALLY MEANINGFUL DREAMS OFTEN OCCUR IN childhood, when a young person is first trying to make sense of his or her place in the cosmos. Childhood spiritual dreams are not marked by any particular imagery or narrative content. They may contain traditionally "religious" themes or characters, or they may appear entirely "secular" and free of any overtly religious imagery.

What really distinguishes childhood spiritual dreams from more ordinary dreams is their *felt power,* an experiential intensity and vividness. It doesn't matter if the child's parents are avid churchgoers, die-hard atheists, or something in between; children from all different religious backgrounds will, from time to time, experience remarkably powerful dreams that express the first stirring of spirituality in their young lives.

Peter was seven years old when he had this brief but very striking dream:

THE BURNING ANGEL

*I saw a burning angel, inside our house near the front
door. Everything was on fire, and the house and the
angel were kind of falling apart in the hot, glowing
flames.*

Although the dream was very short, it felt incredibly
powerful to Peter. He couldn't quite understand what it
meant, but he knew at a deep, wordless level that the
dream was revealing to him something important about
the world. The dream was like a glimpse of tremendous life
energies, at once radiantly beautiful and terribly destructive. "I felt I should be scared of the fire in my house,"
Peter said, "or sad about the angel falling apart. But more
than anything, I felt amazement as I watched those fiery
flames, so bright and vibrant and alive. After the dream, I
always had this special confidence inside me that I knew
about the secret of the fire; even if no one else could see it,
I always knew it was there, very close to me." More than
forty years later, Peter could still remember every detail of
this strangely haunting dream.

Helen was seven when she had a similarly striking spiritual dream. But while Peter's dream included the traditionally religious figure of an angel, Helen's has no formal
religious symbolism:

MOVING SPHERES

*There is a triangular cluster of spheres moving very
fast through dark, starry space. I know that the
spheres are moving, yet as I look they appear to be
standing still. I'm perplexed that the spheres are both
in motion yet standing still, but it doesn't bother me.*

As I look at the spheres, I feel in touch with something good and peaceful.

Helen's remarkable dream is described in psychologist Edward Hoffmann's book *Visions of Innocence*, which contains reports of several other spiritually significant dreams people experienced during childhood.[1] Helen, now an adult, says this dream was "absolutely vivid—in fact, more clear than ordinary, waking consciousness." She once described her dream to a science teacher, who explained to Helen that if she were moving at the same speed as the spheres, they would paradoxically appear to be standing still; in other words, her dream was an accurate portrayal of what it would be like to be moving at the speed of light. As with Peter, Helen never forgot her childhood dream, and it became a touchstone for spiritual reflection throughout her adult life.

Experiences such as Peter's and Helen's indicate that the earliest experiences of spirituality can emerge at a surprisingly early age. Childhood dreams that cause an unusually strong feeling of power can be a person's first encounter with the sacred and can initiate a lifelong spiritual journey.

Dreaming and the Sacred

Spirituality can be defined as a living sense of the sacred, a deeply felt experiential relationship to the ultimate powers of life and the universe. Whether this relationship is described in Judeo-Christian terms as the presence of God, or in Buddhist terms as the Enlightened state of Nirvana, or in Native American terms as a harmony with the spirit beings of the natural world, the sense of connection with powers and energies transcending the ordinary sphere of human existence is the essential core of all forms of spirituality.

Religions, philosophies, and mythologies throughout history have taught humans various practical methods and techniques for becoming more closely connected to the powers of the sacred. Although the world's religious traditions differ in many important ways, one thing they do agree on is that dreams can be a valuable source of spiritual experience, insight, and understanding. This is not to say, however, that all dreams involve profound spiritual revelations. Most religious traditions teach that the majority of our dreams relate simply to the worries and concerns of our ordinary daily lives. But they also teach that spiritual dreams are different. They bear a special vividness, power, and clarity, sharply distinguishing them from "normal" dreams. Although relatively rare, these extraordinary spiritual dreams give people an unforgettable experience of what it means to be connected to the sacred.

However, it is important for parents to recognize that not every childhood spiritual dream is happy or pleasant. A common misconception in our society is that spirituality is all sweetness and light, a realm of purely positive, joyous fulfillment. What we often forget is that the spiritual path is often filled with dark shadows and terrifying dangers, and that any journey along that path requires facing, and overcoming, these fearful elements. Parents should be aware that for children, deep spiritual revelations can be extremely frightening experiences.

When Karen was between the ages of six and twelve she had the following recurrent dream:

GETTING LOST IN THE CAVE

It's a sunny day and I go into a cave with some other children and we try to find something. I become separated from the others, and get lost in a maze of pathways and ledges. It is wet and cold in the cave and I know it's getting dark. Then a giant man is after me and I'm running and running and screaming and crying to get away from him. I wake up just before he can get to me.

Karen always had trouble getting back to sleep after this dream, because she was afraid that if she did fall sleep again she would go back into the dream and the giant man would catch her. Karen had been brought up in a family whose religious beliefs always emphasized the grace and goodness of God. This one-sided spiritual upbringing did not prepare her for the possibility that there might be darker, more destructive aspects of life. It was only through her frightening dreams of the giant man in the dark cave that she was initiated into a broader awareness of how the world is filled with both good and evil forces. Interestingly, Karen's dream echoes the common mythological theme of the "descent to the underworld" as a path of spiritual growth and discovery.

Karen went on to grow up and enjoy a very successful and fulfilling career as a nurse in a hospital pediatrics ward. As she cared for the children in the ward, her recurrent nightmare became a continuing source of insight into the experiences of sick or injured children who were struggling with terrible pain, disorientation, and loneliness. She found that those dreams, as frightening as they were, gave her a firsthand experience of what the children in her ward were going through. She couldn't always make their pain go away, but she could at least join with them in facing those dark, terrible fears.

A similar childhood dream revelation was experienced by Carl Jung, the psychologist who has so deeply influenced modern attitudes toward the spiritual potentials of dreams. The first dream Jung could remember came when he was between the ages of three and four, living with his sternly Protestant family in a small village in the Swiss countryside. In the dream, Jung discovers a hole in the ground, and he walks down along a stone stairway until he reaches a curtained-off enclosure. He pushes aside the curtains, and finds a magnificent throne, with a huge thing like a tree trunk sitting on it:

THE MAN-EATER

It was a huge thing, reaching almost to the ceiling. But it was of a curious composition: It was made of skin and naked flesh, and on top there was something like a rounded head with no face and no hair. On the very top of the head was a single eye, gazing motionlessly upward. . . . The thing did not move, yet I had the feeling that it might at any moment crawl off the throne like a worm and creep toward me. I was paralyzed with terror. At that moment I heard from outside and above me my mother's voice. She called out, "Yes, just look at him. That is the man-eater!"

As Jung says in his autobiography *Memories, Dreams, Reflections,* he never forgot this childhood dream.[2] His frightening vision of the "man-eater" in the cave showed him that Lord Jesus, whom Jung had been taught to worship and obey, was *not* the only power in the universe: "Through this childhood dream I was initiated into the secrets of the earth." As happened with Karen, Jung's childhood dream revelation became a lasting source of inspiration in his adult career as a healer of people's suffering.

Shamanic Calls and Vision Quests

Many of the world's religious traditions pay special attention to children's dreams precisely because a child's special spiritual destiny may first be expressed in an extraordinary dream experience. In some cultures, the dreams of a child may be the first indication that the child is called to be a shaman, witch doctor, or tribal healer. Among the Sambia people of New Guinea, for example, the dreams of children are regularly examined for indications that the spirits have chosen a future shaman.[3] A Sambia girl named Kwinjinaambi dreamed that her deceased mother came to her and told her which herbs and leaves she had to gather in order to perform individual healing ceremonies. When Kwinjinaambi told her father the dream, he recognized it as a "call" to her from the spirit world inviting her to become a shaman. Because of this dream, Kwinjinaambi was chosen by the tribal elders to learn their secret healing traditions, and in time she became one of the most powerful shamans of the Sambia community.

In other religious traditions, children are given specific instructions for seeking out spiritually revelatory dreams. Many Native American cultures practice the ritual of the vision quest, in which an adolescent leaves the village and goes out into the wilderness to fast, pray, and sleep until a special dream occurs. This is the account of a vision quest by a boy from the Ojibwa people, who lived in the hills and forests north of the Great Lakes:[4]

> ### THE GOLDEN EAGLE
> *When I was a boy I went out to an island to fast. My father paddled me there. For several nights I dreamed of an* ogima *[chief, superior person]. Finally he said to me, "Grandson, I think you are now ready to go with me." Then* ogima *began dancing around me as I sat there on a rock and when I happened to glance down at my body I noticed that I had grown feathers. Soon I felt just like a bird, a golden eagle.* Ogima *had turned into an eagle also and off he flew toward the south. I spread my wings and flew after him in the same direction. After a while we arrived at a place where there were lots of tents and lots of "people." It was the home of the Summer Birds.*

At the end of his dream, the boy learns that the *ogima* would be his lifelong guardian spirit and would come to help him whenever the boy needed aid.

These traditional spiritual practices regarding children's dreams are based on solid psychological wisdom. No matter what the cultural setting, the transition from childhood to adulthood is very difficult. A young person must somehow develop a strong, stable personal identity that is true to his or her own unique individuality and yet is recognized and appreciated by the broader community. Dreams are a perfect resource for this difficult developmental task, because through their dreams, children express their most profoundly personal insights into themselves and into the universe. If the community formally honors those dream insights (as the Sambia, the Ojibwa, and many other tribal cultures do), the result is a smooth transformation of a child into a mature, self-confident, and communally engaged adult.

Dreams and Family Religious Beliefs

In families that are actively involved in a particular faith community, the children are very likely to have dreams that reflect their growing understanding of what their family's religious beliefs are all about.

Ted was raised in a Protestant household, but throughout his childhood he paid little attention to his family's religious beliefs. By the time he reached adolescence, he felt confident that true spirituality could be found in many different places, not just in the Christian church. But when he was sixteen, Ted had this short, intense dream:

JESUS COMES TO ME
Jesus Christ came to me and told me that no one could get to the Father but through him.

The dream was, Ted said, "a major theological turning point" for him. It didn't turn him into a raving fundamentalist who scorned all other spiritual practices; rather, it made him realize that, for him, the path to true spirituality lay in the Christian church, the church of his family. The dream helped to integrate his budding individuality with the traditional roots of his family. Several years later, Ted decided to enter a seminary, and he eventually became a Christian minister.

The figure of Jesus also appeared in the dream of a nine-year-old girl named Mary from a religiously conservative family in a small rural town. In Mary's dream, as described in Robert Coles's book *The Spiritual Life of Children,* she was walking through the woods and got lost.[5] After hours of wandering through the dark forest, tired and hungry, she came to a house. A strange man, who looked like Elvis Presley, answered the door. He had a banjo in his hand, and he offered her candy—Milky Way bars, Mary's favorite—as many as she wanted. For a moment, Mary was thrilled, but then suddenly she became scared and asked for a telephone to call her mother and father. The man laughed, said there was no phone, and then started playing his banjo. Mary got so scared she started crying; and then, all of a sudden,

THE PEACE OF JESUS

I see the door open, and there is a flash of light outside; it's like lightning, and I think it's Jesus. He's come to help me. We go outside, and he says you should be careful where you go, or you can get lost, or you can slip and fall, or you can just go around and around in the woods, and you don't find the right way to get you home. And then I woke up, and I was shaking.

Mary told this remarkable dream to her mother, who asked the minister at their church what it might mean. The minister reassuringly said that God had come to save Mary from temptation; she had been "lost," and He had "saved" her. Mary's own interpretation, however, was simpler, and humbler. She saw the dream as a gift, a call to remember what's important in life, and not worry about what's unimportant. She said, "In church, they talk of the 'peace of Jesus,' and I think I was given some of it that night." Her dream took the somewhat abstract religious teachings of her family and her community and made them relevant to the particular worries and concerns of her nine-year-old life.

Many aspects of religion can be quite frightening to children—the rituals, the dramatic stories and myths, the costumes. As young children learn about the traditions of their family's religion, their first reaction is often one of fear. Sometimes, a dream can be one helpful means of overcoming that fear and becoming more comfortable with the family's religious beliefs and practices.

Lucy was a seven-year-old living in a Hindu community. As she grew up, she was always afraid of the old Hindu men, with their white robes and turbans. Whenever she saw one on the street, she would turn around and run home as fast as she could, trembling and shaking the whole way. One night she dreamed that one of these white-turbaned Hindu worshipers was in her room; she ran and ran in the dream, and finally woke up screaming. Lucy's parents took her nightmare as a sign that she needed some special attention and comforting. The next day, her father brought Lucy to meet a friendly Hindu elder, who explained to her why he wore the special robes and turban. Feeling safe with her father right next to her, Lucy got to ask this man all the questions about the Hindu faith that had worried and perplexed her for so long. By the end of their talk, Lucy had to admit that at least some of the men who wore the white turbans and robes were pretty friendly after all.

Many religious traditions have special rituals aimed at introducing children to the adult community of believers. As children prepare for these ceremonies their dreams often turn to imagining what the rites of passage will bring and how their new status as church or synagogue members will change their lives. A few days before his bar mitzvah, twelve-year-old Brad had these two dreams.

I'M LATE FOR MY BAR MITZVAH

I'm driving in a Porsche (our family actually has a minivan) to my synagogue. We are running late and somehow I know there is a three- or four-year-old kid there trying to cover for me until I arrive. I read my portion from the Torah but forget to read my own speech. At first, no one notices. Finally, people realize I have forgotten my speech; for some reason it's too late for me to give it now, and the congregation gets mad and starts throwing tomatoes at me, and I wake up.

I FORGET "BARUCH"

I forget how to pronounce the Hebrew word Baruch, *which is the first word in most of the Jewish prayers and is also my Hebrew name.*

Brad is the youngest child in his family, with three older brothers having already successfully completed their bar mitzvahs. In addition to the celebration of his own bar mitzvah in just a couple of days, Brad had several other things he was worrying about the night of his dreams: homework, student council meetings, the state spelling bee finals, and the school play in which he had the lead role. The day before the dream, Brad had been talking with a friend during class about Porsche sport cars, and their teacher had sternly reprimanded the boys for not paying enough attention to their lessons. Brad's two dreams weave all these stressful elements into an upsetting vision of inadequacy and public scorn. While dreams about performance anxiety are quite common, dreams like Brad's point to the special worries that may be generated by a child's religious rite of passage. Usually, such dreams do more than simply mirror a child's anxieties; they also point to possible sources of strength and resilience. In this case, the key dream element is the Hebrew word *Baruch,* which means "blessed" or "praised." By highlighting the significance of that word, the dream is reminding Brad that he does belong in the Jewish tradition, and that despite his worries he is truly a blessed member of his religious community.

Dreaming of Death

As we discussed in chapter seven, the death of a family member or friend can be a devastating emotional experience for a child, one that reverberates powerfully through their dreams. Here we want to highlight another feature of children's dreams surrounding death: the profound spiritual insights that such dreams provide.

A three-year-old boy named Sam was told by his parents one day of the death of his grandfather, and the loss deeply saddened and upset him. Soon after the grandfather's funeral, Sam had this dream:

THE SNAKE MONSTER
I dreamed there was a snake monster inside Grandpa's back, and it broke out and killed Grandpa.

Sam's grandfather was not really killed by a snake—he had died of a long-term degenerative disease. But Sam didn't understand what a "disease" was, and he didn't understand why his grandpa was suddenly dead, buried alone in a box in the ground. In his short, extremely intense dream Sam wrestles with one of the most profound spiritual questions of human existence: What is death? Religious traditions down through history have tried to answer that question by means of mythological stories and theological doctrines. For three-year-old Sam, his question about death is answered by a dream whose vivid imagery and harsh truthfulness rivals any of the teachings of the world's great religions. Death is something like a snake monster—powerful, mysterious, ferocious, tearing the people we love away from us forever.

One of the most striking types of spiritual dream experience is the startling appearance in a dream of a person who has recently died. In many religious traditions, these dreams are taken as compelling evidence that the human soul lives on after the body's death. The reason why the soul of a dead person will appear in a dream is usually to deliver a special message of warning or guidance; the dreamer is in some kind of trouble, so the dead person comes to offer spiritual counsel, reassurance, and companionship.

Jerry was eleven when his grandfather died, and as he

entered puberty he became increasingly rebellious and hostile toward his family.[6] But then one night he had a very vivid dream:

MY GRANDFATHER COMES BACK

My grandfather appeared and spoke to me. He gently but firmly asked many direct questions about my conduct. At first I started to reply defensively, but then I knew that he was right about every point. It was like no other dream I had ever experienced.

Jerry says that when he awoke he felt that his grandfather had really come to guide him, and he decided right away to break off his association with a crowd of "bad boys" at school.

Did the soul of Jerry's grandfather really come back in this dream? Or was it rather a deeply cherished image of his grandfather within his own unconscious that arose in Jerry's dream that night? It's impossible to answer such questions, and ultimately it's not important. What is important is the effect this amazing dream had on Jerry. He says, "The dream may have been a turning point in my life, for soon after, I began studying more seriously and changing my attitude about a lot of things." Whether or not we believe in religious doctrines about life after death, the extraordinary spiritual effects of dream visitations from the dead are real, and should be honored as such.

Parents should not forget that the majority of children's dreams about death and dying are metaphorical rather than literal. Many dreams with death imagery in them are not necessarily about a "real" death but are symbolic expressions of something "death like" in the child's life.

Jon was a fourteen-year-old who all of a sudden began dreaming constantly about death—about people dying, about animals dying, about dead bodies covering the ground, on and on and on. Jon's mother wondered what all these morbid death dreams could possibly mean—until she looked more carefully at what was going on in Jon's life. In recent weeks he had shown a noticeably greater interest in helping with household chores; he was keeping his room clean, doing the dishes, walking his dog twice a day, all without the usual reminders from his mother. She also found a paper in Jon's room with a carefully written list of "resolutions" he had made for himself to get his life priorities in order. His mother realized that Jon was taking a major step into mature, independent, self-motivated adulthood—and in the process, leaving a big part of his responsibility-free childhood behind. In a very real emotional sense, Jon's childhood was "dying" and his new adult personality was being "born." Once his mother understood this metaphorical meaning of "dying" in his dreams, she was able to talk with Jon and help him with the complex, ambivalent feelings of excitement and sadness that accompany any process of growth and maturation.

The vast majority of dreams about death and dying have this kind of metaphorical or symbolic meaning. But sometimes, very rarely, a dream will come that seems to accurately anticipate a real death. No one can predict when such dreams will happen, and no one knows where they come from, but on those few occasions when they do happen, they can utterly transform a person's spiritual understanding of life and the world.

When the German philosopher Friedrich Nietzsche was five years old, his father died of a painful brain disease.[7] A few months later he dreamed that he was at a funeral, and out of an open grave rose his father, covered in a shroud. His father went into the church, took a small child into his arms, and then climbed back into the grave. Nietzsche told his mother about this terrifying dream, and she comforted him as best she could. But then, a few days later, Nietzsche's younger brother took ill. The child suddenly went into convulsions, and a few hours later he died.

A dream like this is, of course, a terrible thing for a five-year-old to experience; such a horrifying revelation would profoundly disturb and frighten any adult, let alone a young child. But having emphasized that truly prophetic dreams about death are extremely rare, we also want to acknowledge that they do indeed occur. While parents may pray that their children are spared such dreams, they should be prepared to help and comfort their children if they, like young Nietzsche, ever brush up in a dream against the more frightening aspects of the sacred.

Lucid Dreams

Lucid dreams are those experiences in which the dreamer becomes aware, during the dream, that he or she is dreaming. Lucid dreaming was "discovered," in Western scientific terms, in the late 1970s.[8] Yet the phenomenon of conscious awareness within the dream state has been reported in various religious traditions throughout recorded history. Indeed, certain schools of Buddhism teach that attaining consciousness while dreaming is an important step along the path to Enlightenment—the spiritual realization that all life is "but a dream," the creation of our own individual imaginations.

For people in our society, the experience of lucid dreaming seems to be relatively rare, although people say that the few lucid dreams they have experienced have been the most amazing, exhilarating dreams of their lives. For reasons that researchers have yet to fully understand, children seem to have more lucid dreams than do adults. It may be that children's minds are more flexible and open to new experiences than are the minds of adults, or it may be that the rapid cognitive development children go through makes them more liable to have dreams with radical shifts of perspective. Whatever the reason, children are relatively frequent lucid dreamers, and their discovery of self-awareness within a dream may, as the Buddhists teach, open up valuable new spiritual perspectives on their waking world.

Cindy was a ten-year-old with an abundant dream life. She made up her own categories for her dream experiences: happy, scary, and weird. In the "happy" category were flying dreams (she had a recurrent flying dream in which cats were walking around in the air with her); in the "scary" category was a dream of being trapped in a maze in the ocean with sharks chasing after her. What Cindy called her "weirdest" dreams, though, were those in which she somehow became aware that she was dreaming. In one instance she was dreaming of drawing a picture, and then was able to see herself drawing the picture. This experience of both being inside the dream, drawing the picture, and being outside the dream, observing herself drawing the picture, struck Cindy as incredibly strange. From a spiritual perspective, though, such a dream might be Cindy's first glimpse of a more enlightened potential for self-awareness—not just creating but consciously creating. The fact that Cindy felt unsettled by this dream makes it no less spiritually significant. As many religious traditions teach, a person's initial encounter with any new form of spiritual understanding usually appears weird or strange, precisely because it challenges the assumptions of ordinary waking consciousness.

As spiritually stimulating as some childhood lucid dream experiences may be, it must be acknowledged that lucid dreams have their own frightening "shadow" side. Parents should be especially alert to times when a child's experience of self-awareness in a dream makes an already frightening nightmare much, much worse. Between the ages of five and nine, Kristin had a recurrent dream of waking up to find warriors from different eras surrounding her bed, pointing their weapons at her. One held a gun, another aimed a bow and arrow, and still another was a knight in full armor with a long spear and sword. In the dream, Kristin would realize she was dreaming and close her eyes, expecting the warriors to disappear. But each time she opened her eyes she found herself still in the dream, with the warriors brandishing their terrible weapons, bending closer and closer toward her. For Kristin, becoming lucid in her nightmares intensified her fears, emphasizing how trapped she was by the warriors.

Are Dreams Temptations from the Devil?

When the subject of dreams and spirituality comes up, some parents become uncomfortable. They ask, But don't dreams come from the Devil? Aren't all the vain, fantastic images of our dreams nothing but the seductive temptations of demons, sent to lead us into sin and impiety? Shouldn't children be warned against their dreams, so that they won't be deceived by the evil lies that the Devil tries to implant in our souls when we lie unguarded on our beds at night?

Many people who are faithful members of the Judeo-Christian tradition have been brought up with these prejudices against dreams. For such people, all the psychological research in the world won't change their minds, because such research can't compete with the religious authority of Scripture and Church tradition. Our response to these people does not rely on psychology, however, it relies on an invitation to these people to look more carefully at what the Judeo-Christian tradition has said over the centuries about dreams and dreaming. We believe that a careful and respectful reading of the Bible does not support the belief that people of religious faith should ignore their dreams or that dream interpretation is a sin (in fact, nowhere in the Bible does it say that dreams are caused by demons or the Devil). The basic message of the Bible about dreams is that dreams are one of the ways to contact the divine. Although a dream may initially appear strange or frightening, a person who has faith and a discerning judgment can eventually grasp its valuable meanings. From Jacob's dream of the heavenly ladder to the dream revelations Paul received guiding his missionary activities, the Bible has affirmed the divine potential of people's dream experiences.

This scriptural message has been heeded by priests, ministers, and rabbis in almost every branch of the Judeo-Christian tradition. We know of hundreds of clergy members from many different churches and denominations who have found dreams to be legitimate and fruitful sources of spiritual guidance and insight. While recognizing that dreams sometimes bring messages that trouble or upset us, these religious leaders believe that such messages ultimately serve to promote our spiritual growth and wholeness.

As we have discussed in this chapter, certain dreams in childhood mark the initiation of a new spiritual awareness and understanding. Parents who are raising their children within a religious tradition need not worry unduly about the alleged demonic influences on their children's dreams. Rather, parents should welcome these dreams as a chance to honor their children's connection to their emerging spirituality.

Childhood Dreams as Spiritual Treasures

Those few, unforgettably vivid dreams that many people remember from their childhood often become lifelong spiritual treasures. Kelly, in his scholarly writings, has termed them "root metaphor dreams" because they provide vibrant metaphorical images of profoundly mysterious spiritual truths and realities. Ben's dream of the golden bicycle, described in chapter two, is an excellent example of a childhood root metaphor dream, in that it has served Ben throughout his life as a source of wonder, inspiration, and guidance.

Not surprisingly, children will oftentimes refuse to share such extraordinary spiritual dreams with anyone, even their parents. It's as if these children instinctively know that they must carefully protect and cherish some of their dreams, keeping them forever safe in the private realms of their memory.

Whether their children are willing to share their spiritual dream experiences or not, parents can be of real help in the process of understanding, exploring, and honoring such dreams. We offer parents the following advice:

First, don't overemphasize the spiritual potentials of dreams. The vast majority of children's dreams relate to the relatively "earthly" concerns of their normal daily lives. It does children no favor to ignore the valuable expressions and insights of their more ordinary dreams by giving excessive attention to the few spiritual dream experiences they may have.

Second, be open to weird, unexpected phenomena in children's dreams. If a child reports a dream of meeting strange spirit beings or traveling to otherworldly realms, don't automatically assume the child is just making it up or is repeating something he or she saw on TV. As the examples described in this chapter indicate, the spiritual energies of children's dreams often express themselves in forms that strike adults as outlandish or impossible. But the goal should always be to heed the child's felt experience, not the parent's expectations.

Third, be particularly open to the emergence of spiritually meaningful dreams during times of change, crisis, or conflict in a child's life. When a child is going through some kind of major life transformation, dreams will often come to express deep spiritual insights and wisdom, enabling the child to better understand the changes he or she is experiencing.

Fourth, do what you can to help children in the process of honoring those special, extraordinary dreams they *do* decide to share with others. As we describe in chapter eleven, there are many ways for children to creatively express and "play" with their dreams, bringing their images and feelings and energies out into the world. But remember: Sometimes, the best way to honor a dream is to allow the child to keep it private. As always, let the child's feelings be the guide.

Fifth, think of ways to help your children connect their dreams with whatever religious or spiritual events, rituals, and teachings are foremost in their lives. For example, pay special attention to your children's dreams during religious holidays, like Easter, Rosh Hashanah, or Ramadan; look for references in their dreams to religious rites of passage, like bat mitzvahs and first communions; and be on the lookout for possible responses in their dreams to hearing new spiritual teachings, perhaps from a biblical story, the Talmud, a Native American myth, or an ancient Greek legend.

Sixth, take some time to reflect on your own beliefs about God, death, the soul, consciousness, and morality. What comes up in your children's spiritual dreams will almost inevitably relate to your spiritual beliefs, whether you're conscious of those beliefs or not. The more aware you become of your own spiritual worldview, the better prepared you'll be to talk honestly and empathetically with your children about their extraordinary dream experiences. Indeed, you might find that by discussing your children's dreams you come to develop a deeper relationship with the mysterious powers of the sacred.

SOCIAL INFLUENCES ON CHILDREN'S DREAMS

TELEVISION, SEX-ROLE STEREOTYPES, AND THE STATE OF THE WORLD

BATMAN AND THE WITCH

I had a scary dream about a witch. Batman was in my dream, he killed the witch.

FOUR-YEAR-OLD TONY DIDN'T LIKE HIS NURSERY school teacher, and he frequently argued with her and challenged her authority over him. At times, he would become so angry at her that he would hit and kick at her. At one level, Tony's dream clearly expresses his fervent wish that he could simply "kill" his teacher, that he could somehow just make her disappear from his life.

But as we have emphasized several times in this book, dreams never mean just one thing; every dream has multiple levels of feeling, meaning, and possibility. In addition to a wish about his nursery school teacher, Tony's dream expresses his identification with Batman, the hero of his favorite television show. The dream also reflects certain expectations Tony has learned at home and at school about the relations between boys and girls, and men and women. And the dream reveals Tony's emerging attitudes toward violence as a means of resolving interpersonal conflicts.

In all these ways, Tony's brief dream uses various images and themes from his social world to help him frame an experience in his personal world. This chapter focuses on how dreams like Tony's are shaped and influenced by social forces, particularly television, sex-role stereotypes, and patterns of violence and injustice that afflict societies all over the world. We believe that if parents can learn to recognize how both personal and social elements are often intertwined in dreams, they will gain a much better understanding of the powerful influence of society on their children's development. Parents may also be surprised to find that their children's dreams express remarkably clear-eyed and insightful perspectives on what the future holds for our global community.

The Social Development of Children

One of the biggest parts of growing up for children is learning how to become a competent, self-confident member of the broader social world. The ability to interact successfully with other people in society is a crucial skill that all children struggle to develop. And it is a struggle—from a toddler's first hesitant efforts to play with other children at a park, to a grade school child's worries about pressure from peer groups and cliques, to an adolescent's anxious experiences learning how to drive a car. Children grow into the social world with a highly emotional mixture of excitement and fear. They eagerly look forward to becoming more socially competent and to getting to do all the wonderful things that bigger kids and grown-ups get to do; but they are also painfully aware of how small and weak they still are, and they worry terribly about getting lost in the impersonal hustle-bustle of that big adult world.

This tension between yearning for greater social involvement and yet fearing it is a major theme throughout the life of any child. Parents often wonder how they can best help their children work through this tension. In particular, many parents wonder how they can help their children deal with some of the more problematic features of our society today. In this chapter we describe some dream-based methods that parents can use to give their children support and guidance in their encounters with three especially troublesome areas of modern society: commercial television, gender stereotypes about "boys" and "girls," and violence against children.

Commercial Television

As any parent knows, commercial television has an incredibly powerful influence on children in our society. According to surveys, many children spend up to eight hours each day watching television, more time than they spend at school. Thanks to relentless marketing campaigns that plaster images of cartoon characters on everything from toothbrushes and underwear to bed sheets, children (and their parents) are persuaded to spend hundreds of millions of dollars each year buying products they see advertised on television. The impact of commercial television on child development has been heatedly debated by politicians, religious leaders, and social scientists, who have been devising new laws and new technologies to try and combat television's worst effects on children. However, it seems unlikely that either laws or technologies will produce meaningful results any time soon. For better or worse, parents are largely on their own in confronting the power of television.

For many parents, the alarm bells really start ringing when they find that their children have begun dreaming of characters from television. When parents discover their children have dreamed of playing with Barney, fighting with the Power Rangers, or romping around inside a Nintendo video game, they worry that their children have finally become so thoroughly brainwashed by television that it's even gotten into their dreams.

There is nothing automatically sinister about a child's having dreams about characters from television shows. As we have emphasized throughout this book, children always dream about the most prominent aspects of their daily lives —their families, their friends, their schools, and, if they watch television, characters from their favorite programs. The simple fact is we live in a society where television is the single most powerful form of cultural expression.

As children grow up and start trying to make sense of the world around them, they inevitably come into contact with television, and they naturally want to understand what this extremely potent cultural medium is all about. Their dreams are an important way in which children engage in this quite normal process of curiosity, reflection, and understanding. Indeed, given the world we live in, it would really be much more surprising if children didn't dream occasionally about something they had seen on television!

Many times, television programs and videos simply provide a stock of visual images that children draw upon to frame their experiences and emotions. When Sophia was two, she graduated from watching "Barney" to her first full-length video, *The Lion King*. She was fascinated by all the exciting drama and vivid imagery in the Disney movie, and she soon began applying its imagery in various realms of her life. For example, she lost her favorite teddy bear, and no amount of searching through the house could locate it. When Alan sadly informed her it was gone, Sophia said, "That's OK, it go up to stars now"—just like in the movie when the Lion King, Mufasa, explains to his son, Simba, that the great kings of the past now live up among the stars. Soon after this, she used *The Lion King* imagery in one of her dreams. When Alan and his wife were awakened one night by Sophia's cries, they ran into her bedroom to find her calling out, "Hyenas in my crib! Can't move, they on top of me!" Ravenous hyenas are, of course, the villains in *The Lion King*, and Sophia's dreaming mind drew upon their images to give a more distinct shape to her otherwise formless fear of the dark.

In cases like this, dreams referring to television and video programs are the natural result of how the mind goes about creating our dreams: taking bits and pieces from things we've seen in our daily lives (like television shows) and creatively weaving them into a form that gives concise, powerful expression to our strongest feelings and emotions. In this sense, videos and television shows are nothing more than one of the sources of raw material out of which dreams are constructed each night.

Having said that, we also want to confirm what many parents know from painful experience: Watching an especially scary or violent television show can lead to a child having terrible nightmares. For example, "Power Ranger" nightmares are very common right now among younger children, thanks to the widespread popularity of that television show. But it's important for parents to recognize that there is no simple, automatic connection between a television program and nightmares. What such dreams mean always depends on the age, maturity, and current life situation of the child. "Power Ranger" shows, with their blaring rock music soundtrack and hyperactive, wildly violent battle scenes, are much too intense for children in the three- to five-year-old range. When children this age watch the show, they often have terrible nightmares. For instance, one preschooler told Kelly he had lots of scary dreams of "fighting Power Rangers all night long." In many ways these frightening, recurrent dreams bear similarities to posttraumatic stress nightmares, in that the children have been subjected to an overwhelming emotional stimulus that they struggle to work through by means of repeated dreams. If a child has a nightmare that directly replays scenes from a violent television program such as "Power Rangers," it's a clear sign that the show has indeed been too much for the child to handle emotionally.

But for other children, a dream about "Power Rangers" or some other "action" show on television might actually be a sign of growing strength and positive adaptation to the social world. Jerry was a six-year-old kindergartner who had the following dream:

FIGHTING THE NINJAS WITH MY FAMILY
There were ninjas in the world, everywhere. They were fighting with my mom and my dad and my

brother and me. I had a big sword, I was fighting the
bad guy.

This violent dream could easily be taken as evidence that Jerry has been watching too much of his favorite television program, "Teenage Mutant Ninja Turtles." The "ninjas" in Jerry's dream are the evil, black-clad bad guys whom the band of four small but courageous Turtles must fight against in each episode of the show. But such a snap interpretation would overlook what the "Teenage Mutant Ninja Turtles" show means to Jerry in the specific context of his current life. Jerry and his family were originally from France, and they had moved to the United States just one year earlier. Jerry was well aware that, compared to most other people in American society, he and his family were relatively short, with unusually round facial features—very much like the short, rounded Turtles from the TV show. Jerry's dream uses this physical parallel to express his feelings of solidarity with his family and his sense of adventure in this new, challenging country. Despite its appearance, the dream was not scary; on the contrary, Jerry described it with excitement and pleasure—he had fun standing shoulder to shoulder with his family, fighting away the ninja bad guys. This dream expresses the positive, adaptive efforts of a six-year-old to become comfortable in a new social world.

It's very easy for adults to become moralistic when hearing dreams like Jerry's—"Couldn't Jerry and his family have found a way to be nice to the ninjas, becoming friends with them rather than fighting against them?" While such virtuous parental sentiments may be well meaning, they can actually have the counterproductive effect of devaluing a child's actual feelings and experiences.

However amoral Jerry's dream may appear, in all honesty he and his family were truly "fighting," struggling hard to make a new life for themselves in a country where they barely knew the language and had few friends. The dream gave a very accurate portrayal of the emotional reality of Jerry's current life, and it offered a playful and encouraging image of how Jerry and his family could not only survive in their new world but flourish together, as a team.

Now, if the dream had terrified Jerry, that could well have indicated a deeper problem, and if Jerry had started fighting with other kids in school as he does in his dream, that could also have indicated a problem requiring active parental intervention. But the mere fact of having a dream of fighting ninjas is not an alarming sign that a child is addicted to television or is suffering some deep emotional maladjustment. Parents have to be careful not to impose the rules of adult morality onto the imaginary creations of their children, whether in dreams or in other forms of fantasy play, for it is precisely through their dreams and their fantasy play that children explore moral rules and conflicts and gradually learn how to get along with other people.

The best rule of thumb, then, for understanding what it means when a child dreams of a television show is, How does the child feel about the dream? Setting aside what an adult might feel, how does the child respond to what goes on in the dream? By focusing on their child's emotional reactions during and after the dream, parents can gain valuable insights into the meaning of a television image or character that appears in the dream.

Kelly's five-year-old son Dylan awoke one morning and announced that "I just had a good dream!":

RESCUING WISHBONE

Mommy and I were at the beach, with Joe and his mom. Wishbone had been taken prisoner and was being held on an island. So Lambchop and Snugglepuss and I went out to the island and used slingshots to shoot rocks at the people who were guarding Wishbone. We fought the guards away and rescued Wishbone, and that was it.

"Wishbone" was Dylan's favorite TV show, about a talking dog who has all sorts of wonderful, exciting adventures. Joe and his mom, Wishbone's owners, are the other main characters in the show. Lambchop and Snugglepuss are characters from a different television program. Again, at first glance a dream like this could be seen as merely the result of watching too much TV. But a closer look at the dream, and at its context in Dylan's current life, reveals a more complex story. "Wishbone" is a live-action program aimed at older children, and its relatively sophisticated plots really challenged Dylan's growing powers of understanding. "Lambchop," by contrast, is a gentle puppet show intended for younger kids; Dylan had watched it several times, and knew it quite well. In his dream, Dylan imaginatively enters into one of Wishbone's exciting adventures and is faced with the task of figuring out how to rescue the captive dog. To meet this difficult challenge, Dylan draws on resources he knows he can rely on, the characters Lambchop and Snugglepuss. The dream thus shows Dylan using something he already understands (the narrative world of "Lambchop") to help him understand something new that he's just learning about (the narrative world of "Wishbone"). Rather than being controlled or brainwashed by television, Dylan creatively uses imagery from television to help him expand and refine his powers of understanding.

By paying close attention to the appearance of TV characters, images, and themes in their children's dreams, parents can develop a better sense of what impact television is having on their children—for good and for ill. In the difficult parental task of trying to find the right balance between letting kids watch too much TV on the one hand and imposing unnecessarily harsh restrictions on TV watching on the other, children's dreams can be a surprisingly reliable guide.

Sex-Role Stereotypes

As we discussed briefly in chapter five, differences between the sexes in dream content begin to appear very early in childhood. At the beginning of the grade school years, girls start having dreams with a greater number of known characters and with more friendly outcomes, while the dreams of boys have a greater number of unknown characters and relatively more aggressive interactions. As children get older, the patterns in their dreams become more like those found in the dreams of adult men and women. Researchers have found the following basic differences in the dreams of men and women:

- Women dream equally of male and female characters; men dream more often of male characters.
- Women dream more often of familiar people; men dream more often of strangers.

- Women dream more often of themselves as victims of another dream character's aggression; men have more physical aggression in their dreams, and are more often the initiators of aggression toward other dream characters.
- Women have about the same number of friendly and aggressive dream encounters; men have more aggressive dream encounters than friendly ones.[1]

These differences are most prominent in the dreams of men and women in American society, although researchers have found evidence of the same basic patterns in the dreams of people from many other countries. Naturally, there is great debate about what such patterns mean. Do these differences in dream content stem from essential genetic differences in the physical and mental constitutions of men and women? Or do the dreams simply mirror long-standing cultural traditions about how men and women should think, feel, and behave?

We don't want to get mired in the nature vs. nurture debates about these research findings. Rather, we want to focus on the practical question of what parents can do when such sex-role patterns arise in the dreams of their sons and daughters. Developing a comfortable sense of what it means to be a "boy" or a "girl" is a major developmental task in the life of any child.

American society has in recent years become somewhat more open and flexible about sex roles, and this has eased the pressure on children to conform to strict definitions of how boys and girls should behave. But ironically, this has also had the effect of making things even harder for children, because they now carry more of the burden of figuring out where they fit in society's rapidly changing outlook on masculinity and femininity.

To help children navigate through this difficult process, finding a way to successfully integrate a child's unique personal identity with the ideals and expectations of his or her community, we encourage parents to look to their children's dreams: exploring the dreams together, discussing the child's feelings about stereotypically "boyish" or "girlish" behaviors, and examining dream images that highlight social pressures and taboos.

Frank was the third boy in a very active, success-oriented family. His older brothers were good athletes, always got good grades, and were popular with other kids at school. Frank's parents were also quite accomplished, his father being a prominent local businessman and his mother a leader in several charity organizations. His parents wanted to provide Frank with the same opportunities they gave his brothers, so they enrolled him in a prestigious private grammar school, signed him up in a youth soccer league, arranged for him to take music lessons, and generally filled his life with fun, exciting activities.

But then, beginning in second grade, Frank started getting into fistfights with other boys at school. At first, Frank's parents thought the fights were isolated incidents. But as the fights became more frequent, and more violent, his parents began to wonder if they might be symptoms of some deeper problem. One night, while they were talking with Frank about an especially bad fight he'd gotten into that day, they asked him what he was feeling right before the fight started.

"I felt frustrated," he said, with a sudden intensity in his voice that surprised his parents.

"What makes you feel so frustrated?" his mother asked.

"That I can't get away from all of them," Frank answered. And then, without any prompting from his parents, he told them about a recurrent dream he'd been having for as long as he could remember, a dream in which he feels exactly like he does whenever he gets into a fight.

I CAN'T GET AWAY FROM THEM

I'm walking on a nice, clean sidewalk. On my right is a tall fence made of thin wooden slats, like from a cartoon. A couple of the slats are missing, and as I walk along I can see through to the other side. Over there the sidewalk is old and cracked and covered with weeds. The scary thing, though, is that there are lots of strange boys over there, walking exactly the way I am—in the same direction, just as fast as I am, staring at me. I start walking faster, and then they start walking faster; no matter how fast I go, they keep right up with me. I really want to get away from them, so I try to run, but they start running, too. I run and run and run, and then I wake up.

Frank's parents could tell right away that this dream was expressing very deep, complex emotions that had been troubling Frank for some time. The dream gave them a brand-new picture of how life looked to their youngest son—trying to succeed like his older brothers, striving to "get ahead" in a competitive world, measuring his progress only in terms of how far he could distance himself from others. No matter how hard he tried in school (or in his dreams) to "get ahead," Frank could never separate himself from "the pack."

Frank, like many boys in our society, had always been taught that success meant "beating" others. And like many boys in our society, when he failed to "get ahead," he could think of no way to channel his frustration other than through physical violence. His dream gave Frank and his parents a brand-new understanding of how this exaggeratedly masculine conflict had already taken root in his still young personality.

Beyond mirroring that conflict, Frank's dream also pointed to a surprisingly innovative way out of the conflict. After talking about the dream for a while, Frank's father said, "You know, the way those other boys go as slow or as fast as you do, it's almost like they're looking to you to 'set the pace.'"

Frank nodded his head, thinking about this different perspective on the dream. "Yeah," he said, "it's like I'm their leader."

With this new insight in mind, Frank and his parents talked about ways that he could do better at school by following his own path; instead of worrying about getting away from the other boys, he could focus on sharing his ideas and abilities with them.

Frank's story illustrates a dilemma faced by many boys in our society: What is the properly "masculine" way to relate to other people, particularly other boys? His dream, with its anonymous male characters and ominous, frightening tone, perfectly mirrors that culture-wide confusion about masculinity, and fits with the basic patterns that researchers have found in the typical dreams of boys. However, for parenting purposes, we want to emphasize the creative dimension of Frank's dream, the way it offers new

perspectives and potential resolutions to the sex-role identity problems in Frank's life. Thanks to the willingness of
his parents to listen carefully and empathetically to his
dream, Frank was able to recognize this creative dimension
and to try a new approach to dealing with the other boys
at school.

Of course, problems with sex-role stereotypes also
plague the lives of girls, particularly as they approach adolescence. In her book *Narcissus and Oedipus*, psychoanalyst
Victoria Hamilton tells the story of Jean, a fifteen year-old
who, in her efforts to develop a sense of properly "feminine" style and appearance, became entangled in a conflict
common to many teenage girls.[2] Like Frank, she had a
dream that both mirrored her difficulties with sex-specific
behavior and pointed to a creative way out of them.

Jean lived with her father and stepmother in a loud,
busy household filled with six younger siblings, four girls
and two boys. Jean's mother was a successful business-
woman who had moved, after the divorce, into a smaller,
quieter house with Jean's oldest sister. At school and at
home Jean always tried to wear clothes that were neat, normal, and straightforward. She thought that her older sister,
who favored huge sweaters and long skirts, dressed like an
"old granny," while her younger sisters, with all their
makeup and jewelry, tried to look like "*Vogue* models."
Jean's goal was to be "in between"—not too baggy, not too
flashy, just right in the middle.

But this effort to avoid the opposing extremes of con-
ventional women's fashion didn't really make Jean very
happy; she was so fixated on not being like her sisters that
she never considered what she herself would like to be,

what form her own way of dressing as a woman might look like.

One night, Jean had this brief dream:

MY FAVORITE BLOUSE
Our maid took my favorite blouse and put it first in the refrigerator, and then in the oven.

In waking life, the family maid at her father and stepmother's house didn't understand very well how to operate the washing machine and dryer. As a result, she had inadvertently shrunk, bleached, and dyed a number of Jean's favorite garments. Several months earlier, Jean had started doing her own laundry so she could make sure her clothes were done the way she liked.

This dream puzzled Jean at first—why would anyone put clothes in a refrigerator or in an oven? But when she took some time to reflect on the dream's metaphorical possibilities (with the insightful therapeutic help of Dr. Hamilton), several important meanings emerged. Refrigerators and ovens are both common kitchen appliances, and both are enclosures holding food; they differ in that the one is extremely cold, while the other is extremely hot. These qualities led Jean to think of her two homes. The home of her mother was quiet and peaceful, yet somewhat sterile, with a sister who dressed as "coldly" as possible. The home of her father and stepmother, by contrast, was loud, busy, and filled with girls eagerly trying to look as "hot" as they could. Jean's clothes, representing her social identity as a teenage girl, had indeed been ruined by becoming caught in the "refrigerator" of her mother's home and the "oven" of her father and stepmother's home.

In waking life, Jean had realized that she needed to take charge of doing her own laundry. Now, with the insights gained from this dream, she realized that she had to take charge of her own sense of personal style and develop her own sense of feminine fashion and social identity.

Because of the intense pressures society puts on teenage girls to look, dress, and act in certain stereotypical ways, it can be extremely difficult for these girls to become comfortable with their physical appearance. Indeed, developmental psychologists have found that many girls suffer a huge drop in self-esteem when they enter adolescence, leading to poor grades in school, social withdrawal, eating disorders, and various emotional problems. Parents of girls who are in or entering the teenage years can help them fight against these social pressures by encouraging them to share and reflect on their dreams. The creative imagery of children's dreams can point the way to the best response to society's sex-role stereotypes: ignoring them, and trying always to follow one's own path, to develop one's own individual identity.

The State of the World

Few parents appreciate how sensitive their children are to conditions and conflicts in the broader social world. Despite well-meaning attempts by adults to shield them from the worst problems facing society, children are often acutely aware of these problems, and their awareness can be clearly expressed in their dreams. Sexism, racism, poverty, terrorism, environmental destruction—these and many other ills plaguing the current state of the world are sometimes the subject of children's dreaming imaginations. In some cases their dreams reveal a poignant sense of fear and despair children feel in the face of seemingly insoluble social conflicts. For example, Edward's dream of World War III, described in chapter five, is, at one level, a symbolic expression of how his family life is coming to an end as he leaves home for college. But at another level, the dream also discloses a deep terror shared by many children in the nuclear age: a terror that the whole world could be blown up at any moment, that all life on the planet could be killed off simply by the pressing of a few buttons. Many people, adults as well as children, have experienced similar "apocalypse dreams" in recent years, and it may be that the incidence of such dreams will increase as millennial fever builds in the final days of the twentieth century.

Not all children's dreams of the state of the world involve harrowing images of global destruction, however. In other cases, children dream of new hopes and fresh possibilities for themselves and the world, envisioning a future of greater peace, freedom, and prosperity. Ten-year-old Pharoah, one of the two boys described in Alex Kotlowitz's moving book *There Are No Children Here*, lived in one of Chicago's public housing projects, a world of almost unimaginable poverty and despair.[3] Gang warfare, drug addiction, police harassment, and rotting buildings were all that Pharoah had known in his life, and seemed to be all he would ever know. But thanks to the special attention given to him by his fourth-grade teacher, Pharoah wins second place in his school's spelling bee. This small victory gives him a reason to hope that he might someday escape the projects, a hope expressed in this dream:

I GET A JOB

I'm a grown man looking for a job, and people down
the street are calling me because they think they might
have a job for me. . . . I get the job, and the people at
work start calling me "the brain."

The dream made Pharoah feel good about himself, and he told Kotlowitz, "I started thinking about if I do be a lawyer or something, then I'd make a better living and my mama be outta the projects." One dream cannot, of course, immediately change the long history of racism, injustice, and neglect that has left Pharoah and his family at the very bottom of our society. But one special dream can perhaps inspire a child to do whatever he or she can do to create a better future, beyond the boundaries imposed by a sadly imperfect social world.

A fascinating academic study of how children's dreams respond to broader social realities was performed by Israeli psychologist Yorum Bilu.[4] He collected more than two thousand dreams from eleven- to thirteen-year-old Jewish and Arab children living in different settings in Israel and the West Bank. These children were, of course, growing up in a society filled with extreme hostility, violence, and mutual animosity. When Bilu examined the dreams of these children, he found that the "encounter" dreams— that is, those in which Jewish children dreamed of Arabs and Arab children dreamed of Jews—were almost uniformly negative. Here are some examples:

KILLING THE TERRORISTS

Three terrorists sneak into our kibbutz. They hit the
sentry at the gate and a few other members, but the

*other kibbutzniks seize their rifles and kill two of
them. The third terrorist takes my friend as a
hostage, but I kill him.—Jewish boy*

I DIE A SHA'IDA

*An imperialist Israeli soldier enters our school. I stab
him with a pair of scissors. He shoots me, and I die
as a sha'ida [martyr].—Arab girl*

Bilu finds that in almost all of the "encounter dreams," the interaction between Jews and Arabs is suspicious, hateful, and violent. He concludes, "the children under study appear to have internalized the contents of the [Jewish-Arab] conflict as well as its affective tone. Since today's pre-adolescent dreamers are the politicians and soldiers of the coming decades, these firm, well-established schemes and images, if taken seriously, bode ill for the stability and persistence of the conflict." However, Bilu does take consolation in those few encounter dreams in which the children envision a more hopeful future:

NO MORE WARS

*I dreamed that peace prevailed between Israel and its
Arab neighbors, and a Palestinian state was founded
in the West Bank. And there was also peace between
Palestine and Israel, no more wars.—Arab girl*

PEACE WITH THE WHOLE WORLD

*I dreamed that the country was serene and secure. We
had peace not only with Egypt but with the whole
world. War has not recurred, and we had peace with*

*the terrorists, too. Disasters have ceased, happiness
prevails in the world. Peace, only peace and tranquil-
lity.—Jewish girl*

No comparable study has been performed in the
United States, but following Dr. Bilu's lead it would certainly be interesting to listen to the encounter dreams of
American children from different racial, ethnic, and economic backgrounds.

There are no simple cures for society's ills. We have
come to believe, however, that paying closer attention to
children's dreams can be a valuable part of the collective
efforts to find a solution to our problems. A greater famil-
iarity with dreams and dreaming can provide children with
an expanded vision, a deepened empathy, and a creative
flexibility that may enable them to do better than their
parents have in transforming their dreams of peace and
justice into waking world realities.

As we enter the new millennium, everyone's thoughts
are turning toward the future. What will the coming
years bring? What new discoveries, breakthroughs, and
transformations lie ahead? What new crises, conflicts,
and problems are waiting to meet us? The only thing we
know for sure is that the world will be very, very different
by the time our children have grown up and become
adults. When our children have reached our age they will
face opportunities and challenges we can scarcely imagine. Many economists, for example, have said that many
of the new jobs in the next twenty years will be in fields
that haven't even been invented yet. The rapid pace of
change in medicine, communications, transportation,
and information processing guarantees that our children

will inherit a world of vast complexity and astonishing diversity.

The overriding task of parents trying to prepare their children for life in the twenty-first century is to help cultivate their imaginations—giving them the power to adapt to new circumstances, to envision alternative solutions to difficult problems, and to enjoy rather than fear the never-ending changes sweeping our social world. Our firm belief, the belief that motivated us to write this book, is that sharing dreams with children is one of the very best ways to nurture their growing powers of imagination. In a very literal sense, our children's dreams today are going to be society's realities tomorrow.

10

YOUR DREAMS ABOUT

PARENTING

HE EXPLORATIONS IN THIS BOOK HAVE MADE YOU, as a parent, more conscious of your child's dreams and of the significance of dreaming in general. Although we have been encouraging you to remember your own childhood dreams as an aid to understanding your child's dreams, we wanted to take a moment to discuss how your dreams of being a parent can help you understand your own emotional processes as you navigate this challenging and rewarding aspect of life. Taking the time to contemplate your parenting dreams will help you hone your parenting skills. We also invite you to use the exercises in the Dream Catcher's Workbook for yourself as well as for your child.

Have you ever had dreams in which your child was injured, abandoned, abused, or in some precarious situation? You can breathe easy because such dreams are a normal part of the parenting experience. Many parents have dreams that exaggerate their worst fears. Believe it or not, most of these dreams serve the function of keeping us on our toes and spurring us on to avoid the mistakes that are caricatured in our dream images.

Although dreams that symbolize the joys and fulfillment of parenting do occur, it is usually the nightmares about children and parenting that tend to grab our attention. These parenting anxiety dreams take predictable forms. The most reliable characteristic is an exaggeration (and/or distortion) of injuries, illnesses, and dangers faced by your child or other children. It is not unusual for parents who are benevolent while awake to be capable of abuse, neglect, or other atrocities in the dream state.

Caroline waited for two lonely years after her divorce before dating. But when she met Stephen, she found it hard to restrain herself from introducing him to her nine-year-old son, Alex. He was everything her alcoholic, ex-husband had not been, emotionally warm, stable, and not afraid of commitment. After three months, when it was clear the relationship was serious, she arranged for a picnic at a local park. Unfortunately, Alex wanted no part of his mom's new beau, and protested adamantly when he was told he would meet Stephen. Although Caroline suspected that Alex would be jealous, feeling that he was losing some of the special relationship he had with his mom after the divorce, she never expected the ferocity of his reaction. She questioned whether the meeting was premature and consulted with friends, but all agreed that the time had come for Alex to meet his mom's new friend.

Bribed with a new video game, Alex finally agreed to go and the event, while not exactly joyful, went reasonably well and Alex even smiled a few times. That night, however, Caroline dreamed that Alex was in mortal danger.

The Fashion Circus
and the Runaway Van

I was driving in our minivan with Alex and I stopped and stepped outside to see some sort of unusual parade. There were balloons and circus animals and acrobats putting on a show like a combination of a carnival and the Olympics, which had just been on television. Then, there were fashion models, some in tennis outfits and others dressed in strange, colorful, fashions. While I was looking at the models and the circus parade, I suddenly realized that the van with Alex in it had started to roll downhill. I ran after it, screaming for help. "Help, my son! Somebody stop that van!" As I ran I could see a look of terror on his face. I woke up screaming just as the van was about to crash into a dump truck.

Even though she knew it was a dream, Caroline felt guilty for days afterward. The dream was so real that she was almost tempted to believe she had actually placed Alex in danger despite her normally cautious driving style. Still upset, she called her best friend to relate the dream and ask for feedback. Her friend immediately suggested that Caroline might be feeling guilty about all the time she was spending with Stephen. She pointed out that they met while playing tennis at a local park and that Caroline had been spending lots of money on clothes since she met Stephen. Caroline was relieved and excited to hear her friend's associations to the dream. That idea really clicked for Caroline, since she had been worried that Alex felt displaced by her new "friend."

As Caroline talked about the dream to her therapist, she

realized many more interesting connections between the dream symbols and her current life. Going to the circus had been a special treat for Caroline when she was a child. When Caroline was in elementary school, her whole family would go to the circus with her cousins and aunts and uncles, and Caroline used to fantasize about running away and living the life of a clown or an acrobat. The dream was a parody on how much attention she was paying to the circus, a symbol of unrestrained enthusiasm from her childhood, and to her clothes and appearance, which Stephen was praising. The implication of the dream was that she was indeed neglecting Alex by pursuing her own pleasures with Stephen.

Strangely, after discussing the dream with a friend and with her therapist, Caroline felt less guilty. The dream did not diminish her concern and caution about Alex's jealousy of her attentions toward Stephen. Instead, she felt it helped her see the whole picture and gave her new ideas about how to introduce the relationship slowly and to continue to be very sensitive to Alex's feelings. One concrete idea that arose from the dream was to take both Alex and Stephen to the circus. She knew that her enthusiasm would be infectious and might lessen some of Alex's fears about getting to know Stephen.

You can think of parenting dreams as a form of parental report card, sometimes a bit exaggerated and distorted but usually right on target. When we wake up and receive our grades, we learn where we have disappointed ourselves by being selfish, losing our temper, giving inconsistent discipline, spending quality and quantity time or letting stresses from work or finances taint our special time with our children. For Caroline, her circus dream exaggerated the issue but eventually helped her focus more on the important mother-son attachment that had grown even stronger since Alex's father had left.

Beth, a thirty-five-year-old mother of three girls, had a series of nightmares that not only gave her insights into issues that were bothering her eight-year-old daughter, Molly, but they helped her understand a difficult period in her own childhood that had been affecting her relationship with Molly. Ever since the birth of her third daughter, Emma, seven months earlier, Molly began having recurring nightmares of being separated from her family and cornered by a wolf with wickedly sharp teeth. When Molly called out for help, no one in the family could hear her. Beth strongly suspected that Molly's dream had to do with feelings of abandonment, which had increased as her younger sister grabbed more of the family's time and attention with smiles, cooing, and crawling. Beth was surprised at the strength of Molly's reaction because she had not reacted as strongly to the birth of her middle sister, Olivia. At that time, her grandmother came to stay with the family and gave lots of extra attention to Molly, which most likely had minimized her jealousy and distress.

Both Molly and Beth were becoming increasingly distraught about the wolf dreams. Molly was afraid to go to sleep and demanded longer and longer stories and rituals at bedtime. She had unearthed her teddy bear from the closet, needed bright lights to sleep, and even asked for a bottle at times when her sister was being breast-fed. Although Beth tried repeatedly to reassure Molly that she was loved equally as Emma, Molly's anxieties and nightmares seemed to increase rather than subside.

After the fourth occurrence of Molly's wolf dream, Beth

began having nightmares as well. After hearing two upsetting items on the evening news, one about atrocities in Bosnia and the other about the American boy who had been shot by bandits while on vacation in Italy, she had the following nightmare:

MOLLY IS THAT YOU?

The police are pulling up in front of our house. It looks like a SWAT team or an army squadron. They are dressed like they are going to quell a riot, with masks and nightsticks. I am in the house, but also it seems like I am observing from nearby. And it doesn't look exactly like our current house. It's shorter and made of cinder block, sort of like the tract homes in the neighborhood I grew up in. The police are running up our walkway in formation like on a television police show. Suddenly, I hear my name on a megaphone. "Beth Barnett, you are under arrest for child abuse." Then I see some medics carrying out a child's body from the house. I couldn't see who it was but the child was wearing a sleeveless summer dress like one I just bought for Molly. I started to scream—"Oh no, Molly is that you?"—and I woke up sweating and screaming Molly's name.

Beth woke up with an unshakable sense of guilt. For a few hours, she felt like a child abuser who had inflicted indelible wounds on her daughter. She blamed herself for wanting and having the third child that seemed to upset Molly so much. She dwelt upon Molly's feelings of jealousy and abandonment and kept thinking about Molly's terror when she had the nightmares of wolves.

In tears, Beth phoned her husband, Jonathan, at work to relate the dream that she was too frightened to tell him that morning. Jonathan reiterated that he, too, was worried about Molly's nightmares and jealous feelings, but he also pointed out what a diligent mother Beth was and how she had insisted on taking one full year off after each child was born even though it put the family under economic stress. Jonathan suggested that the dream was an exaggeration of her worst fears about Molly's distress and not a realistic portrayal of Beth's mothering skills.

Although Jonathan's suggestions were brief, they were incredibly reassuring to Beth. She called a friend from her mother's group to discuss the dream and Molly's reactions. Her friend confided that she, too, had occasional nightmares about her kids getting injured in accidents. Her friend referred Molly to complete the Dream Catcher's Journal to get help in resolving her wolf dreams.

The more Beth talked about her nightmare, and pondered Molly's waking distress, the more she began to remember experiences from her own childhood. Beth, too, was the oldest in her family with three younger siblings, ranging from two to ten years younger. Beth had gone through years of feeling jealous each time a new sister or brother was born. Beth's mother was a doctor who went back to work within three months after each birth, and although they always had full-time baby-sitters, Beth had to help out with caring for her younger siblings. By all outside standards, Beth was not neglected, but she always had hurt feelings simmering inside that the younger kids got all the attention and that her mom didn't pay enough attention to her. In fact, Beth's own decision to take a full year off after each child was born was an attempt to protect her children from the jealousy that Beth had suffered as a child and to provide a higher level of attention and care than her own mother had provided to her.

Molly's wolf dreams and Beth's own nightmare helped Beth see that her own childhood feelings of being displaced were reemerging. Beth was sympathizing with Molly's anguish but also grappling with her own unresolved conflicts about being the older sibling who had been taken for granted. With this realization, Beth dissipated the dark clouds of guilt toward Molly and began to take constructive action. She read some books on sibling rivalry, talked about the issues with friends, and finally made a plan that included Beth and Jonathan each spending special "alone" time with Molly. She arranged separate dates for bike rides and movies—favorite activities for Molly. She also decided to make a concerted effort to talk with Molly soon after she expressed feelings of jealousy or being neglected.

Most parents don't realize that dreams featuring endangered babies and children are common and may even be a sign that they are working out a conflict related to parenting. Dreams exaggerate and distort issues as a way of dramatizing them. Knowing this can help you dispel the lingering guilt that you will be arrested for child abuse (such as in Beth's dream) or suffer profound guilt for abandoning your child (such as in Caroline's dream).

Parenting anxiety dreams can point objectively to immediate emotional or physical dangers the child is facing. More often, however, they are a caricature of the parent's fears for their child, their doubts about their own behavior as a parent, or a painful recall of issues unresolved from their own childhood. Exploring parenting anxiety dreams can help parents find new ways of resolving how their own inner conflicts interfere with their ability to effectively parent. If you use parenting anxiety dreams to pinpoint problematic issues and concerns in your relationships with your children, you can resolve lingering issues from the past and become more emotionally available for your children.

Dreams and the Parenting Cycle

Although anxiety dreams about parenting are common, not all parenting dreams are upsetting. In general, the themes of parents' dreams follow the crucial events of the parenting cycle from pregnancy through the empty nest and on to grandparenting. Through our dreams we can get insights into our deeper feelings about the stages and changes of parenting from the prenatal fantasizing about how your child will look and relate to you, to the ambivalent feelings of disciplining a rebellious teen, to the mixed feelings of loss, relief, and pride as your child leaves home for college. Each developing capacity, each time they become more independent, each time they anger or disappoint you, will cause dreams and nightmares that can give you clues as to how you are handling your role as a parent.

Pregnant Dreams: The Formation of Your Attachment to Your Child

During pregnancy, parenting dreams take control of your unconscious and shape an inner process of preparation. Dreams, both directly and symbolically related to pregnancy, babies, the birth process, and nurturing a child, occur almost on a nightly basis. Pregnant mothers dream of fertility—fields with rich soil or even flowers sprouting from their breasts. Expectant fathers dream of feeling left out and searching for a role in the pregnancy. They also express their excitement through recurring dreams of "birth"day parties with raucous celebration and lots of cake and other food being served.

Dreams related to parenting begin in the parent's own childhood. Before you knew about "the birds and the bees," you may have heard about the cabbage patch or the stork or had fantasies about babies coming out of belly buttons to escape from their mommy's tummy. These early fantasies may reemerge for expectant parents (paralleling their childhood dreams and fantasies) in the form of babies popping out of the ocean, being delivered by birds or arriving fully developed and playing a mean game of soccer.

Expectant parents frequently dream of giving birth to fish, amphibians, furry mammals — sea otters, kitties, and puppies. Many of these fetal identification dreams symbolize the parent's preparation for parenting, with the endearing animals symbolizing a cuddly and needy newborn. Fetal identification dreams are symbolic snapshots of the beginning of the bond between parent and child.[1]

Dreaming of giving birth to a sea otter was not comforting to Jennifer, who was in her last trimester of pregnancy. She worried that it was a bad omen or a premonition of something abnormal about her baby.

THE SMOOTH SKIN OF THE OTTER
I'm in labor and I am lying on a beach. The tide is coming in and big waves are washing up onto the shore. I keep calling for my husband. I know he's

there, but I can't see him. The waves are getting big-
ger and more dangerous. Just when the waves seem
like they are going to drown me, I see a little sea otter
next to me. I know it was supposed to be my baby, but
I am confused that it looks like an otter. I touch its
skin and it is incredibly smooth.[2]

When Jennifer shared her dream in a workshop on the psychology of pregnancy for nurses and childbirth educators, there were many looks of recognition, because they, too, had dreams of water and giving birth to various animals. They too had anxiety dreams about birth defects and harm coming to their babies. As Jennifer listened to the responses to her dream, she felt relieved and more open to exploring the symbolism in the dream.

Within the dream, there was imminent danger—the big waves that often symbolize labor late in pregnancy. In addition, she was separated from her husband, unable to make contact with him—perhaps feeling alone in the experience and pain of birth.

By sharing her dream, Jennifer realized that she was like other expectant parents in having anxious dreams and fantasies about the well-being of her child. By exploring the feelings in her dream with others, she had discovered her own joyful expectation of holding and caressing the tender flesh of her baby and of bonding emotionally with her child.

Even expectant fathers dream of being pregnant and giving birth as they, too, form an inner bond with their child during pregnancy. Dreams of defending a baby or even a fetus are also common for men and show the mixture of anxiety and powerful paternal feelings of protectiveness. One man dreamed that he was carrying his baby fetus under his shirt with his hands cupped over it to protect it from being attacked by a threatening person. The dreamer then goes ballistic—defending his vulnerable fetus by picking up the attacker and throwing him down in the street.

These and other pregnancy nightmares do not necessarily predict disaster. As upsetting as they are, the presence of anxiety dreams may even be a positive sign that the person is actively coping with the emotional demands of pregnancy or other challenging moments in the parenting cycle. In the case of pregnancy, dreams not only exaggerate the psychological and physical dangers of pregnancy and childbirth but also show a healthy process of inner preparation, with animals or babies in danger stimulating parental feelings or protectiveness and nurturance. In that way, pregnancy and other parenting dreams force us to rehearse for the roles we face, such as caring for a newborn or learning when to let go when an adolescent rebels.

Dreams That Celebrate the Joys of Parenting

While we have emphasized how dreams exaggerate problems related to the parenting cycle, dreams also express parents' profound joys. Parents who only occasionally remember dreams are more likely to recall only nightmares and distressing dreams such as the ones we have discussed earlier in this chapter. Parents who pay more attention to their own dreams will discover a mixture of themes with some portraying deep feelings of affection and pride and a sense of how fulfilling one's role as a parent gives life a more profound and spiritual sense of purpose.

In some dreams the joy of parenthood is delicious. In Alan's study of the dreams of expectant fathers,[3] one of the dominant themes late in pregnancy was dreams of feasting at birthday banquets replete with toasting and celebration. In writing these dreams down and sharing them, many of the men were surprised to discover just how excited they were about the impending birth of their child.

Another class of dreams, especially common for expectant parents and parents of young children, is what we call the "wunderkind dream," where your child performs verbal or physical feats that would surely qualify them for the Olympic trials, if not immediate, lifetime membership in Mensa. An example is one father who dreamed of his first son, a toddler who was just learning to walk in waking life, pitching a no-hitter in Little League. His elation at seeing his infant son stand up and cruise the living room had ignited proud fantasies about his son's athletic prowess.

Wunderkind dreams may emphasize positive hopes as a way of coping with anxieties about the present or near future. For example, wunderkind dreams of expectant parents offer a fantasy leap into the future, past the dangers of labor and delivery, past the diapers and sleeplessness of infancy, and ahead to a time when we fancy that our child will communicate with us in meaningful ways and impress us with their talents.

A twenty-eight-year-old mother who had deferred graduate school and career to have a family dreamed that her first-grade daughter, who was just learning to read, was discovered to be a prodigy and was admitted to the University of California (her mother's alma mater) at an early age. In this case, admiration of her daughter's ability to read signs and books and write stories was so exhilarating that her dream promoted her not just to the head of the class but right through school to college.

These wunderkind dreams express the pride and the hopes of parents who imagine greatness for their children. And what better person than a parent to dream big and inspire a child to his or her highest potential?

The shadow side of wunderkind dreams is that many of these dreams embody more than a little bit of the parent's aspirations as well—the father's dream of his little all-star pitcher was mixed with memories of his own athletic successes and failures, and the mother's thwarted academic aspirations were projected into a dream of her daughter's intellectual accomplishment. Therefore, a wunderkind dream can provide an opportunity to visualize your highest hopes for your child, but may also help you realize whether your unfulfilled ambitions may be imposing a vision on your child that does not fit the child's unique talents.

Most wunderkind dreams help us celebrate and relish our pride in each and every new development in our children, from the emergence of language and communication in the toddler years to the development of artistic, athletic, musical, social, and academic skills later in childhood. Such dreams also help us focus on the intersection of our own aspirations and how they may or may not mesh with the actual talents and aptitudes of our children. In other words, are you projecting your own (fulfilled or unfulfilled) fantasies of grandeur onto those that may work well for your child's unique talents? The consequences can be your disappointment, and a failure to see and encourage your child's special talents.

Generational Dreams

A final category of parenting dreams have a spiritual quality and evoke images of how our children bring us close to
the essence of life and death, the passage of time and generations, and the importance of our mission as parents in
the preservation of our families and our culture. These
"generational dreams" can be joyful, hold a mystical power,
or be bittersweet.

Doug, a forty-year-old father of one daughter, was experiencing grief after the death of his own father. One month
after his father's death he had a dream that helped him
understand both his grief and the profound connection he
had to his father and to his daughter.[4] He dreamed that he
was holding his daughter in his arms and feeling fearful.
Suddenly he saw "blinding" light in a nearby room that
was the "brightest place I have ever been to in my life."
Sensing that it was where his father had gone in death, he
was nearly paralyzed but had to go to the other room to
see if his father was still there. When he heard his daughter
crying, he was "terrified." This dream was both excruciating and illuminating in that it showed him the pain of his
loss and the enduring power of his connection with his
father. At the same time, he felt the dream indelibly
impressed upon him how vital his role would be as father
to his own daughter.

For those parents whose own parents have died, generational dreams often portray the deceased parent being present and seeing some important talent or event in the life of
the grandchild. Although these dreams may accentuate the
grief and longing of the dreamer, they also give spiritual

sustenance when we see how our children and their growth and development is connected to the love and attention we received from our own parents and other family members.

Dreams Enhance Parenting Skills

Multiple benefits can accrue to parents who pay attention to their own dreams, past and present. The enduring power of an adult's childhood dream memories can help parents empathize with their children's dreams and understand lingering issues from their own childhood that may affect their parenting style. They can even sort out where their own issues may be obscuring their ability to understand their children's needs. Furthermore, the impact of a parent who shares dreams is that his or her children will become more relaxed and open about sharing dreams.

Even parental anxiety dreams that portray wildly exaggerated dangers and injuries to children can lead directly to breakthroughs on issues that are distressing or challenging to the family. Moreover, the very nature of dreams is that they exaggerate dangers to our children as a way of stimulating us to discover and rehearse solutions to enhance our ability to protect, nourish, and guide them.

11

THE DREAM CATCHER'S
WORKBOOK

OR CENTURIES, PARENTS IN MANY NATIVE AMERICAN tribes have made "dream catchers" to hang over the beds of their children. Carefully constructed out of twigs, feathers, colored beads, and animal skins, the dream catchers were designed to ward off bad dreams. According to one legend, dream catchers were given to Native peoples by the Spider spirit. Spider instructed humans to hang the dream catcher over their children's beds. During the night, bad dreams would be caught in the magical webbing, slide off, and dry out in the morning sun. Good dreams would go through the hole in the center and fly up to the Great Spirit.[1]

In the morning, tribal parents would ask if their children remembered any dreams, and teach them how to draw guidance from their night visions. Native American children learned to create special songs, dances, and masks inspired by their dreams, to use their dreams as guides in hunting and fishing, and to listen carefully for the call of animal spirits who come in dreams to reveal secret wisdom and tribal lore.

Throughout this book we have mentioned a variety of

techniques for family dream-sharing, drawn from the practices of traditional cultures as well as from the research of
modern psychologists. This chapter explains how to apply
these methods, with variations for different age groups and
family configurations. The methods can be woven into the
ordinary routines of any family, enabling the creative, healing powers of dreams to enrich the lives of both children
and parents.

As we delineate the many methods for remembering,
sharing, and exploring dreams and creating a Dream
Catcher's Journal, we recommend you test them and
choose the ones that work best for your child and your
family. Some children may be more inclined toward artwork as a way of expressing dreams, while others may
enjoy writing, play-acting and drama, or group discussion
and sharing. The best results may come from combining
these methods to more fully express a dream. Trust your
intuition, experiment freely, and have fun—the surest
proof that a dream-sharing method is working is when
both parents and children are enjoying themselves.

Getting Ready

Many parents wonder what they should do if their children
can remember only a few fragments of their dreams; they
worry that their children aren't trying hard enough, or are
suffering some kind of emotional block, or are just not very
creative. We offer the following reassuring facts.

First, everyone dreams throughout the night, during
four to six dream periods that get longer and longer as the
night goes on. Some researchers estimate that we have at
least 150,000 dreams during our lifetime. Children actu-

ally dream more frequently than adults. So if you or your child don't remember lots of dreams right away, don't worry—there will be many more chances!

Second, no special credentials or advanced training is required to remember dreams. All it takes is a little practice, a little patience, and a willingness to let the unconscious respond at its own pace to your interest in its nightly productions.

And third, almost all dreams have rough edges and weird exaggerations. So don't be surprised if your children's dreams seem confused, bizarre, or vague. Much of the strangeness of dreams is due to their special language of symbol and metaphor. Your goal is to become more fluent in the language of your children's dreams. Our experience has been that every dream, no matter how nonsensical it first appears, is a potentially valuable source of personal discovery and creativity.

Probably the biggest obstacle to helping children remember, understand, and appreciate their dreams is what psychiatrist Montague Ullman has called "Dreamism"—the widespread social prejudice against the importance and value of exploring dreams, the unconscious, and our inner world.[2] Dreamism can begin to influence children at a remarkably early age. They might hear an adult at school or on television say something like "Oh, that was just a dream!" or "Dreams are just nonsense!" Such comments might sound innocuous, but we have to remember that children are still in the process of learning about their own inner worlds; when an adult dismisses the importance of dreams, it sends children the message that their dreams and thus their feelings, wishes, and fears don't really matter. As parents, we can combat Dreamism by reviving the ancient art of remembering dreams and making them a part of our daily conversations with our children, family, and friends.

What Is a Dream?

So how do you get started? A wonderful first step is to ask the following questions (relevant for kids of all ages):

- What is a dream?
- Where do dreams come from?
- Why do we have dreams?
- Where do dreams take place?

You may be surprised by what your child says in response—adults often forget that children are continually developing ideas and theories to explain to themselves what they see, feel, and experience in the world. By discussing the above questions, children are encouraged to reflect on the strange, mysterious experiences of their dreams. In the process, parents are given excellent insights into the special ways their children conceive of dreaming.

Psychological research has found that younger children generally do not have a sharply defined notion of where a dream ends and waking reality begins. A four-year-old might say that "dreams are when something funny comes in your room at night," while a seven-year-old might say "dreams are pictures and stories that happen in your head while you're sleeping." It's important for parents not to impose the "correct" adult answers on children. Children should be given as much space and freedom as possible to ponder these questions—as with any other educational subject, it's better for children to learn how to generate their *own* answers rather than having adults tell them how and what to think.

Discussing the nature of dreams can be done in group settings as well. You can gather family members—children, parents, grandparents, cousins, whomever—and ask these questions, letting the youngest family member go first. Someone, an older child perhaps, can write down the answers. Remember to emphasize that there is no one correct answer and that each person can have his or her own definition.

Parents should be alert to those times when their children are wondering about the nature of their dreams but are not able to put their questions into words. Children may have difficulty articulating very complex questions, so it's up to parents to pick up hints—a perplexed frown, a hesitant comment, a fidgety body movement—that may be signaling a child's desire to talk about his or her dreams.

If you discuss these basic questions about the nature of dreams with your children on a somewhat regular basis, over the years you will have the deep pleasure of watching the ever-increasing richness, depth, and sophistication of your children's imagination and self-understanding.

Pretending to Dream Exercise

For very young children (preschool and early elementary school ages), we have developed a role-play exercise that works well in stimulating dream recall and enthusiasm about family dream-sharing.

In this exercise, the child takes a few minutes pretending

to get ready for bed, with all the normal rituals that go along with that process: putting on pajamas, brushing teeth, gathering favorite stuffed animals, climbing into bed, reading a story, and so on. Then, after the pretend lights have gone out and after a few moments of pretend sleeping, the parent says softly, "We're all having dreams now, and when we wake up we're going to try and remember them." The parent allows a long, quiet space of time for the child's imagination to wander. Then, with a gentle word about it being time to wake up, the pretend lights are turned back on, and everyone shares a pretend dream.

This exercise focuses children's attention, in a playful, age-appropriate fashion, on preparing to remember and share their dreams. The interest you show in your children's "pretend" dream experiences will generate excitement and will encourage them to be more sensitive to the dream images they remember in the morning.

What Do People Dream About? Exercise

A different discussion exercise can be used with older children and teenagers to stimulate dream recall and to help make them more aware of their dreams. The following questions are more sophisticated than the ones in the What Is a Dream? exercise and are aimed at prompting older children to reflect more carefully on their memories of past dreams:

- What was your favorite dream?
- What was your worst nightmare?
- Have you ever had any dreams or nightmares that came more than once?

- Did you ever have a dream or nightmare after seeing a scary movie or TV show?
- Have you ever been chased in a dream?
- Have you ever had a dream of flying?
- Have you ever dreamed of being naked, with lots of people around?
- Have you ever dreamed of being in a car crash, or a plane crash?
- What's the strangest dream you have ever had?
- Do your friends or relatives tell you their dreams?

In discussing these questions, parents should encourage their children to explore their remembered dream experiences only in as much detail as they care to. For example, if a child recalls a frightening dream of a plane crashing, the parent might say, "That sounds really scary. What was the plane like?" or "Wow, that sounds terrible! Were there any other people on the plane?" Usually, children will, with just a little parental nudging, go on to describe their dreams in surprisingly elaborate detail. But don't push—it's important for parents not to cross the line from being encouraging to being demanding or intrusive.

Older children (and even some younger ones) may become increasingly guarded about their private lives as they grow up. This can make discussing the personal details of their dreams with their parents an uncomfortable process—"No way I'm going to tell Mom and Dad about *that* dream!" This is a normal development, and the best thing parents can do is simply continue sharing their own dreams with their children. It demonstrates in a very concrete way that you trust and respect your children, and that you remain open to hearing about their dreams.

It's important for parents to be open and reassuring, to create an atmosphere of safety and security, and to avoid the temptation to "interpret" their children's dreams. There's no quicker way to dampen a child's interest in dreams than by saying something like, "Oh, a plane crash dream? You must have had that because we read a book about planes."

Six Keys to Improving Dream Recall

Extensive psychological research has been done to determine what methods work best in improving dream recall. We have summarized below the six most important techniques that both children and adults can use to remember more of their dreams.

1. Create a bedtime ritual that includes concrete steps to prepare you to remember your dreams. Keep your dream journal (or a dream pillow or dream catcher for younger dreamers) close to your bed. Dreams are sensitive to the interest shown by our waking consciousness, and your bedtime preparations send a message to your unconscious that whatever dreams come forth that night will be heard, appreciated, and valued. Before you fall asleep, repeat the following phrase to yourself: "Tonight I will have a special dream and write it down in the morning."

2. When you awaken, before you get up or talk, catch the images that linger from your last dream period by lying quietly in bed. It's more difficult to remember the fragile, fleeting images of your dreams if you jump right out of bed when you wake up. Some people find it helpful to keep their eyes closed and stay in the position in which they

were sleeping. Any dream, no matter how fragmentary, is valid!

3. As soon as you can, grab your dream journal and jot down a few notes and phrases about your dream, or share it with someone else. As you begin to write or tell your dream, more details from the dream will probably come to you. For children under ten, parents should play the role of dream scribe.

4. For younger children, a good technique is to have them write a note to their dreams and put it under their pillow. The note might say something like, "I hope I have a wonderful dream tonight." Parents can help their children compose and write their note, leaving it there (hidden from the tooth fairy, of course) for as many nights as needed. Older children or adults can use the same technique to ask a more important personal question and try to have a dream that gives them insight or guidance.

5. If you or your children continue to have trouble remembering your dreams each night, try returning to the last dream you recall. Share that dream and use some of the techniques listed below to explore its feelings and meanings. This will almost certainly help break the dream logjam and restart the flow of remembering.

6. Share your dreams with trusted friends and relatives and take the time to listen to their dreams. This will create an enjoyable social exchange and create strong interest and motivation to remember dreams.

If, however, dream recall does not come easily, don't put pressure on your child. The world of dreams has its own laws, rhythms, and purposes; no one should try to force themselves (let alone their children!) to remember more dreams. The voice to follow here is the one that guided Kevin Costner in *Field of Dreams:* "Build it, and they will come." Make all the preparations you can, create and color a dream journal, discuss common dreams, make a dream pillow or dream catcher, and then be patient and sleep. The dreams will come.

Sharing Dreams: Telling and Listening

Sharing stories and sharing dreams have much in common. With both, you have to set aside the demands of "reality," stretch your imagination, and surrender to the flow of the narrative. If you and your child have spent any time reading books together, you are already well prepared to share dreams. The same conditions for enjoyable story-reading also work for dream-sharing: sitting or lying together in a comfortable place, forgetting the rest of the world for a while, and joining in the exploration of a fascinating series of images, characters, and events.

Indeed, if your family has ever read the dream adventures of the rebellious Max in Maurice Sendak's *Where the Wild Things Are,* or of the inquisitive Alice in Lewis Carroll's *Alice in Wonderland,* you've got a kind of dream-sharing experience under your belts right now. We suggest that you and your children follow your own dream adventures, which may turn out to be stranger than anything that happens to Max and Alice!

Basic Guidelines for Sharing Dreams

Based on our experience in leading dream-sharing groups with both children and adults, we believe these are the best principles to use in sharing dreams with children in a family context.

Welcoming the Dream: Express a sense of wonder, delight, and curiosity as you listen to your children's dreams. Recognize each dream as a special communication. Encourage and reassure them if the dream is frightening or confusing. Defer interpretation and try to stay with the experience of the dream, inviting playful discussion of all the ideas, memories, and experiences the dream evokes.

Telling and Retelling the Dream: Give your children your full attention and allow them to tell their dreams in their own words. Encourage them (but don't insist) to speak in the first person, present tense—instead of "There was a big horse, and it ran on the beach," say "I see a big horse, and it's running on the beach." This heightens the dramatic tension of the dream, making it more "real" and "present," and thus making the feelings and meanings more accessible. It also helps if the dreamer retells the dream one or more times. This usually triggers the recall of more details and emotions in the dreamer, and will help listeners get a clearer picture of the dream in their minds.

Empathize with the Feelings in the Dream: Children, especially young ones, are often unable to verbalize the complex, forceful emotions that surge forth in their dreams. A child may describe a dream with only one or two simple images—"My teddy bear was in the car, and the car drove away"—but underneath those images are powerful concerns, fears, or desires. Parents need to be alert to the difficulty that young children may have articulating their dream experiences and to empathize with the feelings in the dream. We have found that the most effective way to empathize with the dreamer is to try and place yourself in his or her "dream shoes." With the above dream example you might ask yourself, "What would it be like if had a dream of a car driving away with my teddy bear?" We strongly recommend that you use the phrase "If it were my dream, . . ." to preface your comments about your children's dreams: "If it were my dream, I'd be scared that I was losing my teddy bear." At the very least, this technique will keep you from inadvertently projecting your feelings onto your children—leading them to look at you quizzically and say, "Why would you be scared? In *my* dream Teddy was coming right back!" But beyond that important protective function, the technique of empathizing with your children's dreams will help you understand all the more deeply their strongest emotional conflicts and concerns.

Breaking the Spell of Bad Dreams: When there is obvious fear or distress connected to a dream, active forms of reassurance will help break the frightening spell of the nightmare, bring the dreamer relief, and make room for creative exploration of the dream. Try both physical reassurances (hugs, gentle back rubs) and verbal reassurances ("You're safe now," "We're right here with you," "The bad dream is gone now"). The younger the child, the more concrete the reassurance needed. For example, if a child still sleeps with a stuffed animal, you can enlist the animal as special "nighttime helper" to deal with bad dreams. Children of all ages find it relieving to hear that others have had similar bad dreams. Let your children know that you, too, had nightmares as a child and that you still do occasionally. Explicitly tell your children that you will help them to work out the fears in the dreams by talking and playing together.

We recommend that you do *not* respond to your children's nightmares by saying something like "Don't worry, it was just a bad dream, it wasn't real." Although such comments may be very well intentioned, they can actually make children's fears worse. When children have a frightening nightmare, they know their feelings are real, as real as anything they feel while awake. If they hear their parents trying to dismiss those feelings as "not real" or "just part of a dream," children can only conclude that their parents don't get it—their parents don't understand what they are feeling inside. We strongly recommend that parents always acknowledge the *reality* of the frightening feelings that children experience in their bad dreams, and concentrate on reassuring their children that their parents are with them now and will keep them safe. For example, if your child describes a dream of fighting bad guys in a big forest, you might ask a series of curious, open-ended questions, such as: "How did you fight against the bad guys?" or "What was the forest like?" or "What do you think those bad guys wanted?" Anything you say that expands on or (in the terminology of Jung) amplifies the feelings and images of the dream will help your child learn more about his or her inner world.

The Dream Catcher's Journal

The best book on dreams is the one you and your child write together.

Wildly original and totally unique to your child, the Dream Catcher's Journal will capture a particular period in your child's life and become a lifelong testament to their imaginative powers. When the cover and pages are decorated with your child's original artwork, the Dream Catcher's Journal will become a treasured document that you will want to keep alongside the photo albums and baby books.

For families just starting to explore their dreams, we suggest an initial, limited period—say, one month—for recording your dreams in your journals. During this period, have everyone in the family try to remember as many dreams as they can. This will allow the whole family to concentrate in a relaxed way on remembering and writing as many dreams as possible. After the first month, see how it goes. If everyone remains enthusiastic, you may continue for as many weeks as you like. If interest wanes, you can keep the dream journals in a visible place and let your children ask for them when they have a vivid or upsetting dream. You can also formally reintroduce the dream journal once or twice a year, during a vacation period or a nonstressful time.

Creating the Journal

Anything from a notepad to a sturdy napkin can serve as the first place a dream is written down. However, we suggest that you help your child design a special journal dedicated to his or her dreams. We offer below a few tried and true approaches to making dream journals, but as with everything else in this chapter we encourage you to experiment and try whatever seems most pleasing to your child.

Decorate a Blank Book: Buy a journal, spiral, or three-ring loose-leaf binder and adorn it with drawings, photographs, stickers, and the like. Parents can assist one child in this process, or the whole family can gather and simultaneously make their own dream journals, mixing and matching from an assortment of supplies (markers, crayons, paint, tape, glue, scissors, or colorful magazine clippings).

Build Your Own Journal: Use white or pastel-colored paper and create a book with staple, string, or glue binding. The cover can be made with a vivid photo collage, or a rugged patch of leather, or a regal, velvety fabric. In general, the more children do to make their journals special, the more likely they will value the journal and the process of remembering and enjoying their dreams.

Electronic Dream Journal: If you or your children are already hooked on computers, you can set up your Dream Catcher's Journal on the computer. Using your favorite word processing program, you can keep it very simple, with each person having his or her own file; each dream can then start a new page. Many software companies have designed writing programs especially for children. Some of these programs allow drawings, photos, and sounds to be incorporated, thus opening up the possibility of a multimedia Dream Catcher's Journal!

For advanced computer users, you can import graphics into the journal or create macros that will instantly start a new journal page or collect and sort the dream titles into a glossary. Using our glossary format (see below), you can categorize the animals, persons, places, titles, and soon use a database to search for all the animal dreams that family members have had in the past year or any other topic that you want to categorize.

Making a Dream Journal Entry

We suggest that no matter what dream journal design you create, you should use the following simple Dreamcatching Net format for each journal entry. This format will help your child express each dream as fully as possible, and provide an ideal basis for discussion, reflection, and further exploration. Younger children (under age ten) will need their parents' help in writing dreams; older children can do it themselves or with supervision.

1. **Date:** What was the day and date of the dream?
2. **The Dream:** Describe everything you saw and everything that happened in the dream.
3. **Feelings:** How did you feel in the dream?
4. **Characters:** Who was in the dream?
5. **Setting:** Where were you in the dream?
6. **Title:** What would be a good title for this dream?

DREAMCATCHING NET

Date of dream:

_____

1. Describe your dream. Include everything you saw or heard.

_____

_____

_____

_____

2. How did you *feel* when you were having the dream? Circle one or more and describe your feeling in words.

Happy?   Angry?   Sad?   Worried?   Curious?

3. Who were the *characters* (people and animals) in your dream? Describe them.

_____

_____

_____

4. *Where* did the dream take place?

_____

_____

5. What is a good *title* for this dream?

_____

"The Dreamcatching Net" is the basic building block of the Dream Catcher's Journal. A model Dreamcatching Net page that you can adapt according to your child's needs and artistic inclinations is found on page 239. This simple format, which consists of a series of five key questions, is designed to elicit the most crucial details of a dream and to serve as a catalyst for discussing dreams with your child.

On page 241 is a sample of a child's completed Dreamcatching Net journal entry, which should give you an idea of how the format works.

DREAMCATCHING NET

Date of dream:

August 16 1996

1. Describe your dream. Include everything you saw or
   heard.

   I was at summer camp. My babysitter
   forgot to pick me up. I walked and
   walked and I came to a girl and I
   asked her mom if she knew the
   way to my house. she said
   "yes" and I walked home with her.

2. How did you *feel* when you were having the dream? Circle
   one or more and describe your feeling in words.

   Happy?   Angry?   (Sad?)   (Worried?)   (Curious?)

3. Who were the *characters* (people and animals) in your
   dream? Describe them.

   Me
   My babysitter — my real babysitter
   The girl — She was nice like a girl from camp.
   The girls mom — she was nice because she helped me

4. *Where* did the dream take place?
   At camp.

5. What is a good *title* for this dream?

   My babysitter forgot me.

Family Dream Glossary

The glossary is an archive (and potentially an index) of categories of dream content including titles, animals, people, places, and common themes in your family's dreams. It will help you remember your dreams for future discussion and comparison and will highlight family patterns in dream symbolism. It can be completed in about one minute during or after the sharing of a dream.

For simplicity, you can photocopy the format we provide (see Dreamcatching Net journal entry form) and keep it in one person's dream journal or in a special family Dream Glossary book. The glossary can also be set up as a chart on a large poster board or oversized paper. This has graphic appeal and can stimulate discussion of prior dreams since it encourages everyone to look for connections and recurring themes.

The Dream Space

Throughout the book, and in our guidelines for sharing dreams and keeping the Dream Catcher's Journal, we have illustrated a playful approach that relies on exploring the emotional and creative dimension of dreaming. This approach relates closely to what Carl Jung described as "dreaming the dream onward."

In contrast to the stereotype of armchair analysis of dreams that emphasizes classification and interpretation of symbols and a generally intellectual orientation, we encourage simulating the experience of the dream itself. We have dubbed this state of consciousness the Dream

Space. You can enter this special mental terrain by simply closing your eyes and opening your imagination.

The most vital pathways for unfurling the wings of your fantasies and entering the Dream Space are the creative arts, such as drawing and collage, drama, dance and movement, guided fantasy exercises, and expressive writing, including creating stories, poems, and dialogues based on dreams.

Your child need not be a budding Picasso or Shakespeare to take his or her dreams onward. The following creative dreaming exercises are designed to be accessible to all ages and artistic levels. Their emphasis is more on cultivating emotional expression and helping each dreamer discover his or her unique inner voice, rather than on producing works that will be critically judged as artistic products. In other words, the emotional healing of the dream work lies in the very process of creating and playing with the dream images.

Dream astronauts can launch their journey into Dream Space with an exercise that is a good starting point for many of the other creative dreaming techniques. It can be applied either on an individual or group basis. Best of all, the Dream Space is accessible anywhere in the world, at any time of day.

DREAM SPACE EXERCISE

1. Choose a dream on which to focus and review as you remember it, or reread the dream you have written in your journal.
2. Close your eyes and open your imagination. As your eyes adjust to the darkness of the Dream Space,

stretch your imagination and allow a cascade of ideas, feelings, and images to flow freely.

3. Focus on your dream and be aware of everything you see and feel and hear and smell and touch.

4. Open your eyes and share what you saw or experienced, draw a picture, or make an entry in your journal.

After practicing a few times, encourage your child to try to remember and reexperience all parts of the dream. When the dreamer opens his or her eyes, carefully review his or her experiences. Affirm the uniqueness and creativity of the experiences, and reassure your child as needed about any frightening feelings he or she may have encountered.

The Art of Dreaming

Art is an ideal medium for expressing the meaning of dreams. Although adults have more developed verbal skills, children are less inhibited and can be richly expressive in their artwork. Sketching, painting, collage, mask and costume making, and photography can all be productive vehicles for dreaming the dream onward.

Elaborate and expensive art supplies are not necessary for dream drawing. Old, stubby crayons and newsprint will work just as well as fancy paints and handmade papers. In fact, we encourage erring on the side of simplicity in dream drawing. Start with art materials and techniques that are familiar or appealing to your child, whether it be a favorite set of markers or a stack of magazines that the family has been collecting for collage-making.

First, use the Dream Space exercise as a warm-up to recall and review the dream. Then, with your children's favorite supplies close at hand, encourage them to draw a dream in any way they desire. As always, encouragement and praise will invite more confident and creative responses.

With the completion of your child's first drawing, you have begun the family's Dream Gallery. The Gallery can be exhibited on a spare wall or bulletin board—even temporarily displayed on the refrigerator. If wall space is limited, a Dream Portfolio can be constructed out of cardboard or poster paper folded or stapled, then decorated, to preserve the dream creations.

A fantastic family or classroom project is what we call the Dream Drawing Game.[3] To play the game, one person tells a dream, while all the other participants relax, enter the Dream Space, and pretend that they, too, are having the same dream. It's helpful to reimagine and tell the dream a second time to let the dream story sink in. After the second telling, everyone quietly draws a picture of the dream, remembering to draw it as if it was their own. Take as much time as needed. Then go around the group, allowing each person to relate their experience of the dream and present and describe their picture. Lay out all the pictures together, tape them to a wall or bulletin board, or post them in your Dream Gallery.

When parents participate in the dream drawings, it will not only be inspiring to their children but may be a liberating experience for the parent. When you set aside your own worries about your artistic talents, roll up your sleeves, and get color stains on your fingers, the family will be sharing a moment of collaboration and creativity.

Dream artworks with simple materials can provide inexhaustible possibilities. Some of the projects we have found most rewarding include:

- Sculpting characters or scenes from your dream with clay;
- Designing costumes for characters and acting them out;
- Making puppets of dream characters with socks or bags;
- Making a dream pillow with images of your dreams painted or sewn onto the fabric; or
- Making a family dream quilt which family members can take turns using.

Dream Writing

A dream is a story created, produced, and directed by the dreamer. Using creative writing, a child can embellish that story, continue it, change the dialogue, or create an entirely new ending. They can simultaneously express feelings, flex their creative muscles, and satisfy their curiosity about their dream. The most appealing dream writing exercises are often the simplest. Simply writing the dream down in the Dream Catcher's Journal can be therapeutic and inspiring. And when a child is encouraged to embellish, change, or continue that story, a magical process of creation can occur.

For children who are oriented to telling and writing stories, dreams are a perfect springboard. For preschool and early elementary-age kids, the parent or caregiver must play the role of scribe. For older elementary students, preteens, and adolescents, depending on the child, the parent can play the role of coach, maestro, or muse.

Specific approaches include turning the dream or part of a dream into a story or a poem. Writing a Dream Dialogue can also make a dream come alive with emotions and meaning.

To create a Dream Dialogue, start by entering the Dream Space and picturing your dream. Then choose two or more characters and create lines for them as if you or your child were a playwright. Don't worry about grammar or composition, just focus on the enjoyment of writing and capturing the spirit of your dream.

Eleven-year-old Leah didn't let on to her parents how nervous she was about beginning middle school; suddenly she had multiple teachers, and there were many new children who hadn't been in her elementary school. During the first week, she had the following dream:

CALICO FOLLOWS ME

I'm in my new classroom but I'm barefoot and in my underwear. My cat, Calico, has somehow followed me to school but she is all muddy like she fell in a puddle. I'm so embarrassed, but nobody seems to notice.

An avid writer, Leah was eager to try the Dream Dialogue. She chose her cat and herself as the characters.

ME: What are you doing here Calico and how did you get so muddy?

CALICO: I followed you 'cause I thought you would be lonely.

ME: Well, I'm not lonely, but I'm really embarrassed that I forgot my skirt.

CALICO: I just thought I would keep you company.

ME: Well, I am glad to see you, but how am I going to explain this to the teacher?

As she was writing, Leah began to laugh. The dream didn't seem as frightening or embarrassing anymore. She said, "I guess I'm more scared than I thought about starting my new school." Leah and her mom laughed together about the mud on Calico, and Leah's mom told her that she, too, has had dreams about being naked or in her underwear. The dialogue allowed Leah to acknowledge and share her fears and get reassurance from her mother.

Appearing naked in public frequently symbolizes being unprepared, embarrassed, or having some weakness or incompetence exposed to others. The probable function of these dreams is to help us focus on and potentially resolve anxieties related to events and relationships that are worrisome. Leah's dreams were working overtime to show her that changing schools was more of a big deal than she wanted to admit. In her dream, both characters, Leah and her cat, were expressing important feelings. These included a sense of not being noticed, the need for comfort and companionship in a lonely situation, and multiple worries about how she will be seen and how she will perform in the new school.

While Leah's dialogue did not show every possible meaning of her dream, it did bring feelings to light that Leah was trying hard to suppress. By revealing those feelings, she made a breakthrough in her adjustment to the anxiety of changing schools.

When choosing the characters for a Dream Dialogue, you can choose not only people or animals, but even objects or places appearing in a dream and give them a voice. If a child is having a hard time getting the dialogue going, try suggesting a few specific questions to pose to the dream figures, such as "What are you doing in my dream?" or "Can you help me understand what is going on in this dream?"

Dream Theater

A dream dialogue can also be used as a script for dramatizing a dream. When drama is used, it is helpful to have an adult coaching or directing the play. Encourage children to play both parts in the dialogue. Some people hear parts of existing or original music or songs in dreams. If you or your child are musically oriented, you may want to make up a brief song or chant about part of a dream and then other family members or classmates can join in singing it.

With or without a script, dreams can be used as a basis for dramatization, dance, and creative movement. If there is a particular movement or body motion, children will enjoy acting out the postures or movements of their dream characters. Movements or the behavior of certain charac ters can be turned into a dance or a ritualized set of movements. For example, eight-year-old Rachel had recurring nightmares of horses. She enjoyed mimicking the romping motions of her wild dream horses and then dialoguing with her parents to help try to tame them. Rachel's parents, who grew up with Mr. Ed and Dudley Do-Right's Nell, enjoyed the horse dialogues as well and were impressed with Rachel's persistence in subduing her wild animals.

There are many variations on Dream Theater. A child can take one or more roles in the dream or cast others in various parts. Although an entire dream can be systematically enacted, often producing a key segment will provide plenty of raw material for a family or classroom exercise.

Savoring the experience of the Dream Catcher's Journal, the family sharing, and art exercises will make you a family that dreams together. And this special form of communication and collaboration through the medium of dreams will nourish the creative spark in children, allowing the inner voice of their feelings to speak and help you to be a wiser and more loving parent.

APPENDIX A

EVERY TEACHER'S GUIDE TO CREATIVE DREAM WORK FOR THE CLASSROOM

DREAMS ARE A SPRINGBOARD TO A PLETHORA OF CLASS-room activities that will enhance creativity, raise children's self-esteem, increase parent involvement, and provide an excellent vehicle for psychologically oriented discussions of feelings, important life transitions, assertiveness, and creative approaches to interpersonal and social problems.

This chapter supplements the creative dream exploration techniques covered in chapter eleven, "The Dream Catcher's Workbook" and the nightmare remedies covered in chapter four. The approaches we describe can be applied by classroom teachers, child-care providers, religious school teachers, camp counselors, learning disability specialists, scout leaders, support group facilitators, and play therapists for children.

The single most important aspect of using dreams in the classroom is that every child's dreams are a unique expression of his or her own feelings, relationships, and life experiences.

Because each dream comes from a child's imagination and because we all have an abundant daily supply, dreams are extremely valuable in affirming a child's pride in his or her own creative and productive powers. When students undertake dream-oriented classroom projects, they are expressing their own inner voice.

Because every person dreams many times each night, and children are subject to more frequent nightmares, convincing children of the importance of dreams and galvanizing their interest in dream-oriented projects is not usually difficult. While most of the techniques presented here involve the creative and expressive arts, the study and exploration of dreaming is also relevant to curriculum development in the biological sciences, literature, health education, psychology, and religious studies.

From Preschool to High School

We have conducted workshops in preschools for children as young as three and four, directing them to talk about their dreams, draw pictures of them, and use Native American dream catchers to ward off bad dreams. The result of these workshops was a dramatic increase in children and parents remembering and discussing dreams at home and with each other and their teachers. Parents were surprised at the complexity and creativity of their preschoolers' dreams and felt more confident to understand and welcome exploration of their children's dreams and nightmares.

In elementary schools, arts and crafts–oriented projects inspired from dreams can take many forms (see below) and include in-class visual art projects, dream-related plays, drama and storytelling, recording dreams along with other journal writing assignments, setting up dream pen pals, keeping a class dream glossary with the most common dream and nightmare themes posted for discussion. Each classroom can have a portion of a wall or a special file or portfolio for dream projects. Even parents can get involved by learning more about nightmares, night terrors, and other sleep difficulties. This information can be presented in handouts or through lectures at PTA meetings. Children of elementary school age can be assigned to watch their sleeping brothers' and sisters' eyelids and see the rapid movement that generally signals that a dream is occurring.

In middle school and high school classrooms, the physiology of dreaming and sleep disorders are relevant in biology courses as well as in health education. Basic facts about the biology of REM sleep and the fact that we dream every night can lead to further explorations of physiological and psychological functions of dreams in humans and mammals and to the nature, causes, and treatment of sleep disorders such as sleepwalking, bedwetting, and narcolepsy.[1]

High school students may want to conduct their own dream research—setting up surveys to determine how often people remember dreams and have nightmares or have recurring dreams and night terrors, and what are common dream symbols (see chapter three for details). Research questions can include: Are there differences between boys and girls, grown-ups and children, members of different cultural and ethnic groups?

High school students may also be interested in learning how different cultures interpret dream symbols and view the importance of dreaming in their cultural life. Parochial school students may want to learn about dreams mentioned in the Bible or in the religious texts of their tradition.

As soon as children enjoy writing on their own, but especially in middle and high school, dreams are an ideal source of inspiration for journal writing and creating stories, poetry, dramatic dialogues, even haiku. See chapter eleven for guidelines for decorating and maintaining a dream journal and see below for additional dream writing exercises.

Dream Craft: Recipes for Dream-Oriented Art Projects

Even the most traditional psychotherapists agree that it is not appropriate to interpret or explain children's dreams. In therapy as well as at home and in educational settings, the use of all forms of creative projects, writing, and dramatization are the state of the art for exploring dreams.

Teachers do not have to be trained in counseling or dream interpretation to use dreams as a ready-made inspiration for classroom projects. It is important to steer clear of interpretations and explanations and to keep the focus on the stories, metaphors, and images that emerge, and to help children find age-appropriate projects to give their dreams a voice and a unique artistic form.

Younger children will do better with more carefully structured art projects with short time limits appropriate to their attention span. Older children, particularly those with more confidence in their writing and artistic skills, may want to undertake more open-ended individual or small-group projects.

Building Magical Dream Tools for Overcoming Bad Dreams

Younger children are especially vulnerable to nightmares at critical times of transition in the school year, such as soon after the school year begins, before a big performance, or if a traumatic event occurs in the community or in the school or classroom. At these times, teachers may want to initiate a discussion about who has nightmares and what kind. This is also a good time to initiate projects that have been shown to be effective in reducing the frequency and intensity of nightmares. (See chapter five for a discussion of "magical tools" and "rescripting" nightmares, including creating alternate endings for repetitive dreams.)

Children of all ages know the value of a teddy bear or favorite blanket for reassurance and banishing worries. When a particularly upsetting dream is shared, making magical tools, such as dream catchers and magic wands, begins the process of breaking the negative emotional spell of a nightmare. Just as children, in their play, attempt to work out issues that bother them, creating actual objects for asserting oneself over the threats in a dream story is simultaneously fun and gives the child concrete steps toward overcoming the fears that sparked the nightmare. The projects listed below can be reconfigured for different ages or classroom situations.

Weave Your Own Dream Catcher:[2] Increasing numbers of parents and children of all ages have embraced the use of dream catchers to ward off bad dreams. Now that dream catchers have made it into mainstream culture, they are frequently seen in earrings and necklaces, dangling from rearview mirrors in cars as well as above children's beds and cribs. There are dream catcher kits available from catalogs and in children's stores. If preschoolers and elementary school children make their own dream catchers, they will not only have an interesting project but will have taken an active step toward mastering the fears that emerge in their own nightmares. If you don't use a commercial kit, experiment with fastening colored strings with tacks or small nails on a thick cardboard circle. Punch holes for younger children or find other ways to create a spider web effect. Purchasing or finding real or artificially created feathers will allow the bad dreams to be whisked away from the dreamer according to legend. The dream catcher can also be decorated with beads, markers, and glitter.

Magic Wands, Shields, Sprays, Quilts, and Amulets: Magic wands and shields can be made of branches gathered from nature, baked ceramics, recycled cardboard, aluminum, wood, or any other objects available at little or no cost. Magic wands can be decorated with sparkles, paint, small mirrors, scented oils, even small flashlights, or enclosed objects to make rattling sounds. Shields, of course, require special symbols and crests painted or mounted in collage format from magazine clippings. A shield or dream catcher can be sewn onto a quilt that can be used individually or made by an entire class and passed around for protection from bad dreams. Amulets can be special stones, crystals, or natural objects either purchased or discovered in nature and used near the bed to magically ward off bad dreams. Once created, magical tools can be used to dramatize imaginary new endings or solutions to bad or repeating dreams. See chapter five for more details on the use of magical tools.

More Dream-Inspired Writing Projects

In the classroom, younger students with emerging printing and cursive skills will take pride in just writing the dream down in a special dream journal that they have decorated as part of a class project. Once it is written down, the dream can be a jumping-off point for other writing projects. In chapter eleven, the basics of creating and maintaining a dream journal and doing dream dialogues are described. What follows is a broader list of writing projects:

- Write a story about what happened before or after the dream.
- Turn a dream into a story written from another character's point of view.
- Create a story that uses magical tools to resolve a dream conflict.
- Compose a poem or story based directly or indirectly on a dream.
- Create a written glossary of dream symbols and themes from an ongoing dream journal.
- Using a dialogue format, turn a dream into a play script that can be performed by classmates.
- Write "free associations" to a dream wherein you picture the dream and write down every thought and feeling that comes to mind using a five- or ten-minute timer.

- Go to the library and do research on a symbol that occurs in one of your dreams, such as a tidal wave, spider, or unicorn.
- Interview others and write down their dreams and their ideas and interpretations.
- Write an essay on artists, writers, and scientists who have been inspired by their dreams.
- Experiment with other writing projects inspired by dreams.

Dream Buddies and Pen Pals: A project that can be organized through a school, scout troop, or friends and relatives is a Dream Buddy or Dream Pen Pal program. A Dream Buddy could be a cousin, a best friend, or a neighbor. For younger children especially, it is best to have parents organize a Dream Buddy program centered around keeping journals or doing art or writing projects together. Phone sharing, letter exchange, or e-mail can supplement formal meetings. It is important that all sharing emphasize an emotionally supportive and playful approach and steer clear of interpretations or judgments about the meaning of symbols.

Electronic Dreaming: As computers become more available in classrooms, dream journals, dream writing projects, and classroom dream symbol glossaries can be kept on disk and become part of learning word-processing skills. Students can bring their journals back and forth from home computers via disk or modem transfer. With e-mail or online chat rooms, students in classrooms around the world can undertake exchanges. Forums for sharing dreams are growing rapidly on the World Wide Web. At the time of this writing, major Internet providers such as America Online have areas that provide both information and interaction on the topic of dreams and the international Association for the Study of Dreams has an educational Internet site with information for parents, teachers, and children; bibliographies; and reviews of dream-oriented books, films, and other dream-related Internet sites.

Dream Themes Hit Parade: An excellent way to promote class discussion of dreams and to invite exploration of the many meanings of dream symbolism is to take a survey of class members, parents, and friends and find out which are the most common dream themes and symbols. It may be disaster dreams, such as earthquakes or hurricanes in an area where one has just occurred, or dreams filled with performance and test anxiety, especially just before midterm exams. The Dream Theme Hit Parade can evoke frequent discussions both in class and at recess and lunch, as well as at home. For older students, researching recurring dreams and common themes could also form the basis for a science class project that compares differences between girls' and boys' dreams or between grown-ups and children or other groups.

Dreams and Literature: Many works of literature feature dream sequences that can provide a basis for discussing many aspects of dreams in the classroom. Appendix B provides an extensive annotated bibliography of dream-oriented books for children categorized by age group. Illustrated with magnificent artwork, many of the works of fiction listed will provide hours of education and enjoyment for in-class and homework reading assignments and book reports.

Come to the Dream Fair

A Dream Fair is a gathering of young dreamers, parents, and teachers to celebrate the full spectrum of creativity that dreams can inspire. It usually involves multiple creative avenues for dreaming the dream onward, including dream-oriented art, writing, theater, and dance.

Although every Dream Fair is different, we suggest the following basic structure: First, you will need a sponsoring group, which could be a classroom teacher, scout troop leaders, the school PTA, or other parents or youth group. It's best to orient the parents a few weeks before the Dream Fair, giving them basic instructions for remembering dreams and keeping a journal. We recommend either using our Dream Catcher's Journal or some variation. Classroom teachers can reinforce the preparation period by talking about dreams in the classroom, or using the exercises presented in this chapter.

On the day of the Dream Fair, each child brings one written dream that they have reviewed at least once with their parents or teacher. At the Dream Fair, workshops and way stations are set up to allow children to express their dreams in as many art forms as they see fit. There can be painting and drawing areas, dream puppet and mask-making areas, stages for dramatizing dreams, story and songwriting workshops, as well as audio or video areas where children can record their dream and describe or film some of their creations. Special materials for making dream journals should always be provided so that each child can leave with a journal that will inspire them to further dream creations.

T-shirts, masks, and puppets can be used for a dream

character parade that could serve as a finale for the event. Younger children can be accompanied by parents or observed in the creative act from a distance. Parents could also choose to participate or to attend a parent workshop on children's nightmares and how to conduct some of the projects at home.

After a Dream Fair, when you eavesdrop on the playground, in the lunch room, and at the PTA meeting, dreams will be a hot topic of conversation and most children and adults will find themselves remembering and sharing dreams more often. After a Dream Fair is an excellent time to continue to "dream the dream onward" at home using the techniques that your child showed the most enthusiasm for at the Dream Fair.

APPENDIX B

ANNOTATED BIBLIOGRAPHY OF CHILDREN'S BOOKS RELATED TO DREAMS

HILDREN'S BOOKS PROVIDE AN EXCELLENT RESOURCE for parents who want to help their children learn more about their dreams. Many of the best works of children's literature are stories specifically about dreaming—about the strange, exciting, sometimes frightening adventures that young heroes and heroines have in their dreams. Children love these stories so much because the fictional stories reflect, explore, and celebrate aspects of their own dream lives, their own adventures in the wondrous realm of dreaming.

Below are some of the best children's books related to dreams, with brief descriptions and commentaries. We suggest that parents think about which books might be of special interest to their child, based on the child's own distinctive dream experiences. For example, a child who has especially wonderful dreams of flying will likely enjoy stories with that theme; a child who has been troubled by nightmares will probably take a deep interest in stories where a young protagonist struggles to overcome frighten-

ing dream foes. As always, we encourage parents to experiment and to listen carefully to the interests, needs, and
desires of their child.

Books Best Suited for Ages Two to Five

Dreams, written and illustrated by Ezra Jack Keats
(Aladdin Books, 1992). One night, while everyone else in
his apartment building is asleep and dreaming, a boy
named Roberto looks out his window and sees an angry
dog threatening his friend's cat. Roberto accidentally
knocks a paper mouse off his windowsill, and as the mouse
falls its shadow becomes fantastically large; the dog is
scared by the mouse's shadow and runs away, and Roberto
happily goes to sleep. This simple story, with its somber,
muted illustrations and sparse text, evokes the dark mysteries of the nighttime, and reassures children that in
dreams even the smallest creatures can have great powers.

The Dream Book, written by Margaret Wise Brown, illustrated by Richard Floethe (Dell, 1990). This is a gentle lul-
laby poem about the ability all creatures have to dream of
what will come in the future. The dreams of squirrels and
bees, rabbits and fish, birds and horses are envisioned here,
with each dreaming of their happiest desires. Like Brown's
other books, *Goodnight Moon* and *The Runaway Bunny,* this
story is aimed at very young children. But its deep wisdom
makes it suitable for older children as well.

When Cats Dream, written and illustrated by Dav Pilkey
(Orchard Books, 1992). This delightful story begins with
the quiet, uneventful life of cats during the day, and then

plunges suddenly into the wild, colorful world of cats dreaming. In this magical world, cats are released to do whatever they wish: They can swim in the sea and gleefully terrorize the fish, dance on the heads of sleeping dogs, dress in socks and ties like humans, and travel back to their ancestral jungles. *When Cats Dream* leads children to wonder what other people, and other creatures, might be dreaming about. Both children and parents will appreciate the artistic shift from the cats' waking world (rendered in black and white, with references to staid classics of art history) to their dreaming world (portrayed in vivid, playful colors, with nods to Picasso and other iconoclastic modern artists).

There's a Nightmare in My Closet, written and illustrated by Mercer Mayer (Dial Books, 1968). This popular book tells of a young boy who is frightened by a nightmare—a large, strangely shaped monster who lives in his closet. The boy tries to fight the nightmare with toy soldiers and pop guns, but is surprised to find that the creature is actually scared of *him.* This story resonates very strongly with young children who are just beginning to understand what dreams and nightmares are like. Mayer's helpful advice is that sometimes we can best overcome those things we fear not by fighting them but by befriending them.

What a Bad Dream, written and illustrated by Mercer Mayer (Golden Books, 1992). One of Mayer's little "critters" falls asleep on his mother's lap, and dreams of drinking a magic potion that turns him into a frightening monster. In his dream, the critter scares his parents away, then does whatever he pleases: eats ice cream for breakfast, leaves his room a mess, never bathes or brushes his teeth, stays up watching TV as late as he wants. But then the critter gets sleepy, and lonely. He finally wakes up, and asks his mother and father to tuck him into bed. Most children will enjoy this cheerful dream fantasy about getting to do whatever we wish, without our parents getting in the way; most children will also recognize the message that our wishes can be scary, too, and can, when taken to extremes, cut us off from the people we love.

The Dream Child, written and illustrated by David McPhail (E. P. Dutton, 1985). The Dream Child, a young girl with light, flowing hair, and her friend Tame Bear go sailing away through the night sky in a boat with wings. They go to meet Tame Bear's mother, the Queen, who feeds and cares for them. They also go into a dark forest, where they find two angry giants (who happen to look a lot like parents). This story's soft watercolor illustrations and gentle poetic text create a serene, peaceful atmosphere that allows children both to enjoy the happy adventures of dreaming and to feel confident facing the sometimes frightening conflicts that emerge in dreams.

Where the Wild Things Are, written and illustrated by Maurice Sendak (Harper and Row, 1963). This classic, Caldecott Award–winning story tells of a rebellious boy named Max who, being sent to bed without supper, falls asleep and dreams of sailing to a mysterious island, where the wild things are. Max becomes king of the wild things, and enjoys dancing and howling and playing in the jungle with his monster subjects. But then he becomes lonely, and sails back to his room, where he awakes to find his supper waiting for him, still warm. No other children's story so perfectly captures the powerful, unruly inner impulses that children struggle to control in both their waking and dreaming lives.

Books Best Suited for Ages Five to Eight

The Boy Who Dreamed of an Acorn, written by Leigh Casler, illustrated by Shonto Begay (Philomel Books, 1994). This book is based on the rite of the Spirit Quest, practiced by many Native American cultures to initiate children into their spiritual traditions. Three boys climb a mountain one moonlit night to search for a dream of power, a dream in which a special animal spirit will come to them and become their lifelong guardian and guide. The first boy dreams of a great bear, the second boy of a mighty eagle, but the third boy only dreams of a small acorn. Although disappointed at first, this boy learns to appreciate the hidden powers within the acorn, and within himself. With its mythologically rich narrative and quiet but luminous illustrations, *The Boy Who Dreamed of an Acorn* is one of the very best children's books available for portraying to children the deep spiritual potentials of dreaming.

The Dream Pillow, written and illustrated by Mitra Modarressi (Orchard Books, 1994). This story draws on the common American folk practice of making dream pillows, using special herbs and flowers to inspire good dreams (see chapter eleven). Two girls, Ivy and Celeste, don't like each other, even though they are next-door neighbors. By exchanging a dream pillow as a birthday gift, and by learning to understand each other's dreams and nightmares, Ivy and Celeste gradually become good friends. The story suggests that sharing and understanding dreams can be an important beginning to true friendship.

The Great Kapok Tree, written and illustrated by Lynne Cherry (Gulliver Books, 1990). A man goes into the Amazon rain forest to cut down a huge, beautiful Kapok tree. He chops at it with his ax, but soon tires and lies back against the Kapok's trunk to sleep. While he sleeps, the jungle animals whose lives depend on the tree come one by one to whisper in his ear and ask that he not cut it down. This book's finely detailed illustrations vividly express the lush beauties of the rain forest. The simple moral of the story—don't selfishly destroy the natural habitats of other living creatures—evokes the power of dreaming to give special insights into the relationship of humans and the natural world.

The Tale of the Flopsy Bunnies and *The Tale of Mrs. Tiggy-Winkle*, written and illustrated by Beatrix Potter (Frederick Warne, 1989). These stories, two of the twenty-three that Beatrix Potter wrote in the early 1900s, touch on the strange and even dangerous experiences children sometimes have while dreaming. In *The Tale of the Flopsy Bunnies*, six little bunnies fall asleep in a pile of mown grass and are discovered by the irascible farmer, Mr. McGregor. As he gently carries them back to his house to cook them for his dinner, the bunnies happily dream of their mother tucking them into bed, oblivious of the danger they are in. The story acknowledges the common childhood concern that sleeping and dreaming are times of great vulnerability. In *The Tale of Mrs. Tiggy-Winkle*, a little girl named Lucy wanders into the hills and finds a pleasant woman all covered with prickles who has been doing the wash for all the animals of the neighborhood. But at the end, Lucy realizes that Mrs. Tiggy-Winkle is nothing but a hedgehog, and she suddenly wonders if she had dreamed the whole thing. Here, the strangely real yet not-real quality of dreaming is evoked. Both stories convey Potter's basic belief, most famously expressed in *The Tale of Peter Rabbit,* that children must balance their experiences of magic and wonder with a realistic awareness of the many dangers present in the world around them.

Jessica and the Wolf: A Story for Children Who Have Bad Dreams, written by Ted Lobby, illustrated by Tennessee Dixon (Magination Press, 1990). Written by a professional social worker, this book is specifically designed for parents who are trying to help children suffering from nightmares. A girl named Jessica is having bad dreams of being chased by a wolf. She tells her parents about the dreams, and they help her develop a plan to stop the wolf. The next time Jessica dreams about the wolf she follows her parents' advice and waves a magic wand at the beast; with the help of her favorite stuffed animal, she then recites a spell that banishes the wolf. This story nicely illustrates the practical steps parents and children can take to transform a painful problem with recurrent nightmares into a positive experience of learning and growth.

The Berenstain Bears and the Bad Dream, written and illustrated by Stan and Jan Berenstain (Random House, 1988). Brother and Sister Bear play with some "Space Grizzlies" action figures, and then go to see an exciting movie about the Space Grizzlies battling the evil Sleezo. That night both Brother and Sister have frightening dreams that weave together various images and feelings from the previous day. They run to their parents' bed, where Mama and Papa Bear comfort the children and explain to them that nightmares aren't real, but are just mixed-up bits of things in your mind. Although this story (one of more than forty books in the Berenstain Bears series) gives a generally accurate picture of how dreams are formed, it still leaves children with the unfortunately rationalistic impression that dreams are basically nonsense.

Free Fall, illustrated by David Wiesner (Mulberry Books, 1988). In this Caldecott Award–winning book told only with pictures, a boy falls asleep in his room and slowly enters a magical dream world where his toys come alive, where he meets fearsome dragons and friendly pigs, and where he flies, falls, and tumbles through strangely transformed bits and pieces of his waking life. Because there are no words to this story, it encourages children to use their own imaginations to understand what the boy is experiencing. *Free Fall* also shows children that some dreams are simply impossible to put into words, and are best expressed in picture form.

Night Visitors, written and illustrated by Ed Young (Philomel Books, 1996). Set in China, this book tells of a young scholar, Ho Kuan, who dreams of living with the ants, learning their ways, feeling their fears and their hopes, and helping them fight their battles for survival. In the end, Ho Kuan discovers that the ants, seemingly the smallest and most insignificant of creatures, in fact have a true dignity and nobility that deserve his respect. *Night*

Visitors illustrates the power of dreams to give us new perspectives on the world, and to help us understand the lives of creatures different from ourselves.

The Nutcracker Ballet, retold by Melissa Hayden, illustrated by Stephen T. Johnson (Andrews and McMeel, 1992). This story (available in many different versions) tells of the dream adventures experienced one Christmas Eve by a young girl named Clara. After falling asleep by the candlelit Christmas tree, Clara dreams of a fierce battle between the Mouse King and the Nutcracker (a toy figure who had been accidentally broken earlier in the day). Clara helps to save the Nutcracker's life and defeat the malevolent Mouse King, and she is rewarded with the discovery that the Nutcracker is really a prince, who leads her to a joyful celebration in the fabulous Land of Sweets. This story has been a children's favorite for more than a century, as it vividly evokes the special magic of Christmas dreams.

Humphrey's Bear, written by Jan Wahl, illustrated by William Joyce (Henry Holt, 1987). Winner of a Redbook Children's Picturebook Award, this story tells of a boy named Humphrey who, despite his father's disapproval, insists on going to sleep with his favorite teddy bear. Humphrey dreams that he and his bear sail away across the sea and enjoy wonderful adventures together. When Humphrey wakes up he realizes he's lost his bear, but then his father comes into the bedroom, finds the bear, and hands him back to Humphrey, saying, "I used to sail with him, too." The book speaks to the conflict all children face between their "babyish" desires and the demands of their parents. Here, the conflict is resolved by parents and children sharing their dreams, by Humphrey's father realizing that he, too, used to have dream adventures with this same teddy bear.

Coyote Dreams, written by Susan Nunes, illustrated by Ronald Himler (Aladdin Books, 1994). At night, a young boy hears coyotes coming from the sandy desert outside his house. He hesitantly goes out to see them, and to his surprise discovers a natural world that's suddenly alive and vibrant. The boy plays with the wolves, sings and dances with them, and learns how to pronounce their ancient name: *coyotl.* This story is a wonderful dream adventure about befriending that which seems in the daylight to be different, alien, and frightening. Through his dream the boy learns that the seemingly barren desert is actually filled with life and beauty.

Just a Dream, written and illustrated by Chris Van Allsburg (Houghton Mifflin, 1990). A boy named Walter thoughtlessly tosses his garbage on the street and can't be bothered with separating bottles and cans for recycling. But one night he dreams of the future, of what it will be like if people don't take better care of the environment: neighborhoods buried under mountains of garbage, forests cut down to make toothpicks, the Grand Canyon lost beneath a blanket of smog. This cautionary environmental fable draws on the real power of dreams to imagine what will come in the future if we don't change our conscious ways. Children will enjoy Walter's ironic, exaggerated dream visions (rendered in Van Allsburg's award-winning artistic style), even as they are challenged to apply the story's moral to their own lives.

Ship of Dreams, written and illustrated by Dean Morrissey (Harry N. Abrams, 1994). At the prodding of his friend Archie, young Joey tries to stay awake one night to catch a glimpse of the Sandman. Just as Joey drifts off to sleep, he's suddenly jerked awake and carried in his red wagon up into the sky. He tumbles out of the wagon and falls in terror toward the earth, but is then caught in the netting of a huge ship sailing through the clouds. Joey is hauled on board by an old, white-bearded man—the Sandman. He graciously allows Joey to join him in his travels around the world, casting his sparkling golden sand down on the eyes of sleepy people everywhere. When Joey wakes up in his bed the next morning, he decides he's *not* going to tell Archie about what he saw. The illustrations in this joyful story are simply stunning, and children will spend hours marveling at Morrissey's renderings of the Sandman and his fantastic flying ship. Many children will also appreciate the book's message that it's OK to keep some dreams private, as personal treasures to cherish all by oneself.

Books Best Suited for Ages Eight and Older

Alice's Adventures in Wonderland, written by Lewis Carroll (various editions). This is the best-known dream adventure in all of children's literature. Young Alice falls asleep one afternoon and tumbles down a rabbit hole to discover a strange world where she meets a most remarkable collection of characters—the White Rabbit, the Mad Hatter, the Cheshire Cat, and, most terrifying of all, the Queen of Hearts. In Wonderland everything Alice has learned at school is turned upside-down, and she wanders from curious incident to curious incident, vainly trying to find her way home again. Although younger children will certainly delight in the comic encounters and mishaps of Alice's tour through Wonderland, the story is really aimed at older children, who are able to appreciate fully the complex and subversive playfulness of Carroll's story.

The Sign Painter's Dream, written and illustrated by Roger Roth (Crown, 1993). Clarence is a grouchy old man who paints signs for a living and who, at the end of each day's work, likes reading history books about the Revolutionary War. A kindly old woman comes to Clarence one day and asks if he would paint her a "free apples" sign to let people know that she's giving away apples from her orchard. Clarence refuses to paint the sign for free, but that night he has a startling dream in which General George Washington comes to him and asks him to paint a sign (for free, of course) to help the soldiers fighting in the war. Clarence wakes up, and immediately paints a huge, magnificent sign for the old woman. This humorous story has likable characters and a gentle, dream-based moral about generosity, kindness, and community spirit.

Tree of Dreams: Ten Tales from the Garden of Night, written by Laurence Yes, illustrated by Isadore Seltzer (Bridgewater Books, 1995). This is a wonderful collection of stories about dreams gathered from cultures all over the world— from Brazil, China, India, Senegal, Greece, and many other places. In one story, a man befriends a magical badger, who returns to help the man in a dream. In another story, a boy dreams of wealth and marriage to a princess, and he wins them both through his remarkable cleverness.

Introduction

1. Alan Siegel, *Dreams That Can Change Your Life: Navigating Life's Passages Through Turning Point Dreams* (New York: Berkley, 1996)
2. F. A. Kekulé von Stradonitz dream and speech as quoted by Stephen Brook, *The Oxford Book of Dreams* (Oxford: Oxford University Press, 1987), 139.

Chapter 1

1. Montague Ullman and Nan Zimmerman, *Working with Dreams* (Los Angeles: Jeremy Tarcher, 1979).

Chapter 2

1. For further information about the role of dreams in artistic creativity through history, see Robert Van de Castle, *Our Dreaming Mind* (New York: Ballantine, 1994).
2. Naomi Epel, *Writers Dreaming* (New York: Carol Southern, 1993).
3. Ibid., 8–9.
4. See David Foulkes, *Children's Dreams: Longitudinal Studies* (New York: Basic Books, 1982).

5. Harold Blau, "Dream-Guessing: A Comparative Analysis," *Ethnohistory* 10, no. 3 (1963): 233–249.

Chapter 3

1. Delaney poses the question in these terms: "Pretend I'm from another planet . . ." See Gayle Delaney, *Living Your Dreams* (New York: Harper & Row, 1979).
2. Denyse Beaudet, *Encountering the Monster: Pathways in Children's Dreams* (New York: Continuum, 1990).
3. From Naomi Epel, *Writers Dreaming* (New York: Carol Southern, 1993), 141–142.
4. Anthony Shafton, *Dream Reader: Contemporary Approaches to the Understanding of Dreams* (Albany: State University of New York Press, 1995).
5. From Epel, 207.
6. Jean Piaget, *Play, Dreams, and Imitation in Childhood* (New York: W.W. Norton, 1962).
7. Ibid., 178.

Chapter 4

1. John Mack, *Nightmares and Human Conflict* (Boston: Houghton Mifflin, 1974), 3–4.
2. Ibid.
3. Lenore Terr, *Too Scared to Cry* (New York: Basic Books, 1989), 210–213.
4. Ernest Hartmann, *The Nightmare: The Psychology and Biology of Terrifying Dreams* (New York: Basic Books, 1984), pp. 102–109, and *Boundaries in the Mind: A New Psychology of Personality* (New York: Basic Books, 1991).
5. Hartmann, *Boundaries in the Mind*.

6. Patricia Garfield, *Your Child's Dreams* (New York: Ballantine, 1984), 290.

7. Alan Siegel, "The Dreams of Firestorm Survivors," in *Trauma and Dreams,* Deirdre Barrett, ed. (Cambridge: Harvard University Press, 1996).

8. Barry Krakow, "Nightmares and Sleep Disturbances in Sexually Assaulted Women," *Dreaming* 5, no. 3 (1995): 199–206.

9. The concept of "rescripting" was adapted from Gordon Halliday, "Treating Nightmares in Children" in *Clinical Handbook of Sleep Disorders in Children,* Charles Schaeffer, ed. (New York, Jason Aronson, 1995).

10. Diagnostic Classification Steering Committee, *International Classification of Sleep Disorders: Diagnostic and Coding Manual* (Rochester, Minn.: American Sleep Disorders Association, 1990).

11. Richard Ferber, *Solve Your Child's Sleep Problems* (New York: Simon & Schuster, 1985).

12. Christian Guilleminault, *Sleep and Its Disorders in Children* (New York: Raven, 1987), and Schaeffer, *Clinical Handbook of Sleep Disorders in Children.*

Chapter 5

1. Sigmund Freud, *The Interpretation of Dreams* (New York: Avon, 1965).

2. David Foulkes, *Children's Dreams: Longitudinal Studies* (New York: Basic Books, 1982).

Chapter 6

1. Patricia Garfield, *Your Child's Dreams* (New York: Ballantine, 1984), 153.
2. Stephen Catalano, *Children's Dreams in Clinical Practice* (New York: Plenum, 1990), 130.
3. Ibid.
4. John Mack, *Nightmares and Human Conflict* (Boston: Houghton Mifflin, 1974), 127–129.

Chapter 7

1. Stephen Catalano, *Children's Dreams in Clinical Practice* (New York: Plenum, 1990), 154.
2. Lenore Terr, *Too Scared to Cry* (New York: Basic Books, 1990).
3. From ibid, 210–211.
4. Alan Siegel, "The Dreams of Firestorm Survivors," in *Trauma and Dreams*, Deirdre Barrett, ed. (Cambridge: Harvard University Press, 1996).
5. Kathleen Nader, "Children's Traumatic Dreams," in *Trauma and Dreams*, Deirdre Barrett, ed. (Cambridge: Harvard University Press, 1996), 14.
6. Carl O'Nell, *Dreams Culture and the Individual* (Novato, Calif.: Chandler and Sharp, 1976), 66–67.
7. Daniel Schaeffer and Christine Lyons, *How Do We Tell the Children? Helping Children Understand and Cope When Someone Dies* (New York: New Market Press, 1988), 52–53.
8. From Catalano, *Children's Dreams*, 127–129.
9. From Nader, "Children's Traumatic Dreams."

10. Ricky Ray was interviewed on CNN television news on January 7, 1993.

11. Marie Louise von Franz, *Dreams and Death* (Boston: Shambhala, 1987).

12. Maureen Sinnott, *Dream Content Differences Between Roman Catholic Women Religious (Nuns) and Married Women During Menopausal Transition,* unpublished doctoral dissertation, California School of Professional Psychology, 1994.

13. John Weil, *Instinctual Stimulation of Children: From Common Practice to Child Abuse* (Madison, Wis.: International Universities Press, 1989).

14. Virginia Woolf, "A Sketch of the Past" in *Moments of Being* (New York: Harcourt, Brace, Jovanovich, 1985); as quoted in Terr, *Too Scared to Cry,* 228–230.

Chapter 8

1. From Edward Hoffmann, *Visions of Innocence: Spiritual and Inspirational Experiences of Childhood* (Boston: Shambhala, 1992), 169–170.

2. C. G. Jung, *Memories, Dreams, Reflections* (New York: Vintage, 1965), 11–12.

3. Gilbert Herdt, "The Shaman's 'Calling' among the Sambia of New Guinea," *Journal de la Societe des Oceanistes* 33 (1977): 153–167.

4. A. Irving Hallowell, *Culture and Experience* (Philadelphia: University of Pennsylvania Press, 1955), 178.

5. Robert Coles, *The Spiritual Life of Children* (Boston: Houghton Mifflin, 1990), 129–137.

6. From Hoffmann, *Visions of Innocence,* 168–169.

7. Ronald Hayman, *Nietzsche: A Critical Life* (New York: Penguin Books, 1980), 18–19.

8. See Stephen LaBerge, *Lucid Dreaming* (Los Angeles: Jeremy Tarcher, 1985).

Chapter 9

1. See Veronica Tonay, *The Art of Dreaming* (Berkeley, Calif.: Celestial Arts, 1995).

2. Victoria Hamilton, *Narcissus and Oedipus: The Children of Psychoanalysis* (London: Routledge & Kegan Paul, 1982), 156.

3. Alex Kotlowitz, *There Are No Children Here: The Story of Two Boys Growing Up in the Other America* (New York: Doubleday, 1991), 188.

4. Yoram Bilu, "The Other as a Nightmare: The Israeli-Arab Encounter as Reflected in Children's Dreams in Israel and the West Bank," *Political Psychology* 10, no. 3 (1989), 365–389.

Chapter 10

1. Alan Siegel, *Dreams That Can Change Your Life: Navigating Life's Passages Through Turning Point Dreams* (New York: Berkley, 1996), 59–94.

2. Ibid, 60–61.

3. Ibid.

4. Ibid, 235–237.

Chapter 11

1. Suzanne Lord, *The Story of the Dream Catcher and Other Native American Artwork* (New York: Scholastic, 1995).
2. Montague Ullman and Nan Zimmerman, *Working with Dreams* (Los Angeles: Jeremy Tarcher, 1979).
3. Henry Reed, "The Dream Drawing Story Game," and Alan Siegel, "Dreaming Together," both appeared in "Art in the Dream Group," *Sundance Community Dream Journal* 1, no. 2 (Spring 1977).

Appendix A

1. Charles Schaeffer, *Clinical Handbook of Sleep Disorders in Children* (New York: Jason Aronson, 1995), and Quentin Regestin, David Ritchie, and the Editors of Consumer Reports Books, *Sleep Problems and Solutions* (Mt. Vernon, N.Y.: Consumer's Union, 1990).
2. Instructions for making a dream catcher are given in Suzanne Lord, *The Story of the Dream Catcher and Other Native American Artwork* (New York: Scholastic, 1995).

RESOURCES

BELOW ARE SOME OF THE BEST BOOKS ON CHILDREN'S dreams, and on dreams in general, that we recommend for further reading. If you are interested in learning more about dreams, we strongly suggest you contact the Association for the Study of Dreams at P.O. Box 1600, Vienna, VA 22183; (703) 242-0062; ASDreams@aol.com). ASD is the world's leading organization devoted to dream research, education, and outreach. They publish an academic journal, *Dreaming;* a magazine, *Dream Time;* and a series of pamphlets on all aspects of dreams. They also maintain an Internet site on the World Wide Web at www.outreach.org/gmcc/asd/

BOOKS ON CHILDREN'S DREAMS

Beaudet, Denyse. *Encountering the Monster: Pathways in Children's Dreams.* New York: Continuum, 1990.

Bynum, Edward Bruce. *Families and the Interpretation of Dreams: Awakening the Intimate Web.* Binghamton, N.Y.: Harrington Park Press, 1993.

Catalano, Stephen. *Children's Dreams in Clinical Practice.* New York: Plenum, 1990.

Ferber, Richard. *Solve Your Child's Sleep Problems.* New York: Fireside, 1985.

Foulkes, David. *Children's Dreams: Longitudinal Studies.* New

York: Basic Books, 1982.

Garfield, Patricia. *Your Child's Dreams.* New York: Ballantine, 1974.

Schaeffer, Charles. *Clinical Handbook of Sleep Disorders in Children.* New York: Jason Aronson, 1995.

Wiseman, Anne Sayre. *Nightmare Help: A Guide for Parents and Teachers.* Berkeley, Calif.: Ten Speed Press, 1989.

GENERAL BOOKS ON DREAMS

Barrett, Deirdre, *Trauma and Dreams.* Boston: Harvard University Press, 1996.

Bulkeley, Kelly. *Spiritual Dreaming: A Cross-Cultural and Historical Journey.* Mahwah, N.J.: Paulist Press, 1995.

Epel, Naomi. *Writers Dreaming.* New York: Carol Southern, 1993.

Hartmann, Ernest. *The Nightmare: The Psychology and Biology of Terrifying Dreams.* New York: Basic Books, 1984.

Kippner, Stanley (Editor). *Dreamtime and Dreamwork: Decoding the Language of the Night.* Los Angeles: Jeremy Tarcher, Inc., 1990.

Shafton, Anthony. *Dream Reader: Contemporary Approaches to Understanding Dreams.* Albany: State University of New York Press, 1993.

Siegel, Alan. *Dreams That Can Change Your Life.* New York: Putnam/Berkley, 1996.

Taylor, Jeremy. *Where People Fly and Water Runs Uphill.* New York: Warner Books, 1993.

Van de Castle, Robert. *Our Dreaming Mind.* New York: Ballantine, 1994.

INDEX

The authors would appreciate hearing your responses to *Dreamcatching.* You can write to them at P.O. Box 9332, Berkeley, CA 94709-0332.

Alan Siegel, Ph.D., is a clinical psychologist who has worked with families and children for more than twenty years in Berkeley and San Francisco. He has taught courses and workshops on dreams for all ages—preschoolers through graduate students—for about twenty-five years and is the author of *Dreams That Can Change your Life*. He is vice president of the Association for the Study of Dreams and editor in chief of *Dream Time,* an international magazine on dreaming. His research projects on the dreams of expectant fathers, trauma survivors, and children has brought him international recognition. He has been featured on *CNN News, Sonya Live,* the Discovery Channel's "The Power of Dreams," and NBC's "The Secret World of Dreams." He lives with his wife and two daughters in the San Francisco Bay area.

Kelly Bulkeley, Ph.D., earned his doctorate from the University of Chicago Divinity School and his masters from Harvard Divinity School. He is the author of *The Wilderness of Dreams, Spiritual Dreaming, Among All These Dreamers,* and *An Introduction to the Psychology of Dreaming,* as well as several articles on dreams, psychology, spirituality, and child development. He is currently president of the Association for the Study of Dreams, the world's leading international organization devoted to dream research and education. His work on dreams has been featured on a number of television programs, including CBS's "This Morning," the Discovery Channel's "The Power of Dreams," and NBC's "The Secret World of Dreams." He lives in Kensington, California, with his wife, two children, and three cats.